C0-DXA-118

R00402 70433

CHICAGO PUBLIC LIBRARY
HAROLD WASHINGTON LIBRARY CENTER

R00040270433

```
LB      Armstrong, Steve W.
2838
.A76    Practical self-
1984      monitoring for
          classroom use
```

DATE			

SOCIAL SCIENCES & HISTORY DIVISION

THE CHICAGO PUBLIC LIBRARY
EDUCATION & PHILOSOPHY

© THE BAKER & TAYLOR CO.

PRACTICAL SELF-MONITORING FOR CLASSROOM USE

PRACTICAL SELF-MONITORING FOR CLASSROOM USE

An Introductory Text

By

STEVE W. ARMSTRONG, Ph.D.

Assistant Professor
Special Education Department
Jacksonville State University
Jacksonville, Alabama

and

GREG H. FRITH, Ed.D.

Professor and Chairman
Special Education Department
Jacksonville State University
Jacksonville, Alabama

CHARLES C THOMAS • PUBLISHER
Springfield • Illinois • U.S.A.

Published and Distributed Throughout the World by
CHARLES C THOMAS • PUBLISHER
2600 South First Street
Springfield, Illinois 62717

This book is protected by copyright. No part of it
may be reproduced in any manner without written
permission from the publisher.

© *1984 by* CHARLES C THOMAS • PUBLISHER
ISBN 0-398-04961-0
Library of Congress Catalog Card Number: 83-24205

With THOMAS BOOKS *careful attention is given to all details of manufacturing and design. It is the Publisher's desire to present books that are satisfactory as to their physical qualities and artistic possibilities and appropriate for their particular use.* THOMAS BOOKS *will be true to those laws of quality that assure a good name and good will.*

Library of Congress Cataloging in Publication Data

Armstrong, Steve W.
   Practical self-monitoring for classroom use.

   Bibliography p.
   Includes index.
     1. Teachers—Self-rating of. 2. Teachers of exceptional children. I. Frith, Greg H. II. Title.
LB2838.A76 1984   371.9   83-24205
ISBN 0-398-04961-0

Printed in the United States of America
PS-R-3

This book is dedicated to my wife, Bobbi, my daughter, Ashley, my parents, and the others who have helped along the way.
Steve

Personal appreciation is extended to my parents, June and George, and my Aunt Ellen for their tremendous support and encouragement.
Greg

PREFACE

Self-monitoring can be meaningful to almost anyone who is willing to make the effort to understand and use it. This includes a wide variety of age groups and developmental levels, ranging from preschool children to senior citizens.

The purpose of this book is to provide classroom teachers with a practical guide for using self-monitoring with their students. The text is written to be easily understood, with examples and vignettes commonly provided to illustrate key points. There are also occasional references to pertinent studies in the professional literature. They are provided to give credit where it is deserved and to emphasize that ideas presented here have a theoretical base.

In addition to being of value to classroom teachers, the text has much to offer school counselors, parents, mental health specialists, practicing psychologists, and others who are concerned with human behavior. In fact, a person with no professional interest in a behavioral discipline may be surprised to discover the text has value to him or her as well. For example, most people are interested in improving some aspect of their behavior, whether it relates to smoking, eating, nail biting, or a variety of other common functions.

In the final analysis, each one of us is responsible for his or her own behavior. Self-monitoring provides us with an excellent tool for systematically accepting this responsibility. The question is, Are we willing to make the effort to learn enough about this process to make it a practical skill within our behavioral repertoire? An affirmative answer could have a significant impact on the quality of our daily lives, as well as on the influence we have on each other.

ACKNOWLEDGMENTS

The authors wish to thank Sandra Dyar and John Hendrix for their assistance in editing and typing the manuscript.

CONTENTS

	Page
Preface	vii

Chapter

Section I: General Principles

1. *Introduction* 5
   - Self-Monitoring Defined 6
   - Purposes of Self-Monitoring 6
     - Assessment 7
     - Therapy 7
     - Initial Stage of Self-Management 8
     - Other Purposes 8
   - Advantages of Self-Monitoring 9
     - Facilitates the Learning of Responsible Behavior 9
     - Allows Observation of "Hidden" Behaviors 10
     - Maximizes Use of Teacher Time 10
     - May Improve Self-Awareness 11
     - Allows Generalizations to Other Environments 11
     - Allows Work on Low-Priority Behaviors 11
     - Affords Maximum Use of General Observational Skills ...12
     - Can Be Introduced Early in the Educational Process 12
   - Self-Monitoring and Individual Differences 12
   - Common Terms 13
   - Conclusion 16

2. *An Overview of the Self-Monitoring Process* 17
   - Operational Definitions of Specific Behaviors 17
   - Types of Behavioral Recordings 19
   - Self-Evaluation with Self-Recording 21
   - Self-Monitoring and Teacher-Monitoring 21
   - Reactivity 22

Page

    Conceptualizing the Self-Monitoring Process 23
        The Consequences of Behavior 24
        Self-Administered Reinforcers 25
        Self-Administered Punishers 26
        Self-Administered Antecedents/Self-Instruction 27
    Conclusion 30

3. *Counting and Recording Target Behaviors* 31
    Identification of Target Behaviors 31
    Counting Devices and Recording Mechanisms 33
    Helpful Hints for Collecting Data 36
    Common Problems and Possible Solutions 45
    Conclusion 51

4. *Special Implications for Exceptional Students* 52
    Mentally Retarded 53
    Learning Disabled 55
    Visually Impaired 56
    Hearing Impaired 57
    Communication Disordered 57
    Physically Handicapped 58
    Behavior Disordered 59
    Gifted and Talented 61
    Conclusion 63

Section II: Specific Applications

Introduction 67

5. *Academic Behaviors* 69
    General Academic Skills 70
        Task-Related Behaviors 70
        Assignment Completion 74
        Study Behavior 77
    Specific Academic Skills 79
        Handwriting 79
        Written Expression 81
        Arithmetic 84
        Reading 86
    Miscellaneous Factors 87
        Self-Selected Versus Other-Selected Contingencies 87
        Self-Instruction 88
    Conclusion 89

Page

6. *Inappropriate Classroom Behaviors* 91
   Introduction to Appropriate Interventions 91
   Self-Rating with Disruptive and Academic Performance 94
   Self-Ratings Without Teacher Monitoring 97
   Managing Aggression and Emotional Control Problems 98
      Young Children, Aggression, and Emotional
         Control Problems 98
      Managing Aggression and Emotional Control Problems
         in Adolescents 100
   Conclusion 102

7. *Personal and Covert Behaviors* 105
   An Introduction to Personal and Covert Behaviors 105
   Advantages of Self-Monitoring Personal and
      Covert Behaviors 108
      Provides an Avenue for Improving Some Private
         Behaviors 108
      Stresses the Student's Role as a Primary Change
         Agent 109
      Allows Generalizations Back to Overt Behaviors 109
   Potential Problems and Possible Solutions 110
      Defining Measurement of Covert Behaviors 111
      Coping with Less Conscious Covert Behaviors 112
      Selecting a Proper Recording Device 113
   Conclusion 115

8. *Vocational and Self-Help Skills* 117
   Vocational Skills 118
   Self-Help Skills 122
   Conclusion 127

9. *Self-Management: The Completed Process* 128
   A Synopsis of the Self-Management Process 128
   Reviewing the *ABC*s of Behavior Change 129
      Behavior 129
      Consequences 130
      Antecedents 131
      Integrating the *ABC*s 132
   Two Types of Self-Management: Cognitive Behaviorism
      and Radical Behaviorism 133
   General Suggestions for Teaching Self-Management 135
   Conclusion 144

References 145

Index 151

PRACTICAL SELF-MONITORING FOR CLASSROOM USE

SECTION I: General Principles

Chapter 1
INTRODUCTION

Behaviorists were the first professional group to develop a systematic approach that individuals could use to observe, record, evaluate, and manage their own behavior. Laymen, however, have often used behavioral techniques without assigning them formal names. A common yet simple form of self-management is the use of a shopping list.

Individuals who purchase groceries frequently are penalized for shopping without a list. One common penalty for shopping without a list is a larger food bill. Another possible penalty is the tendency to buy impulsively. Punishment resulting from lack of a systematic plan is often called *response cost*. Another punisher frequently encountered by shopping without a list is the verbal (or nonverbal) response received from other family members after returning from the store without a particular item. To avoid these penalties, individuals are strongly encouraged to shop for groceries with a predetermined list. Unfortunately, most of us are not as systematic in coping with other common needs in our lives.

An extension of the shopping list example occurs when shoppers cross out or check off the items on their list as they are placed in the shopping cart. For individuals who experience positive reinforcement upon completion of grocery shopping, the check-off practice can be self-rewarding by providing evidence of task completion. Also, some items on a lengthy list may be forgotten without a systematic recording system.

The process of crossing off items after putting them in the grocery cart is a form of self-recording or self-monitoring. Most of us have learned this behavior by observing someone else with a shopping list, or at least listening to someone describe how one is used, experimenting with use of a shopping list and/or experiencing the consequences of shopping both with and without a list.

Another common example of self-monitoring is to compile a written list of tasks that need to be accomplished within the next day. As behaviors are completed, they are checked or crossed off the list. Similarly, some individuals rely on pocket calendars to plan daily responsibilities, often covering a month or a year at a time. Others write daily lists of behaviors on small notecards or notepads. As stated earlier, the marking of these tasks as complete can be reinforcing in itself. Individuals who use these types of selfmonitoring are frequently referred to as reliable, efficient, organized, or structured.

Self-Monitoring Defined

According to Mahoney and Thoreson (1974), successful self-control procedures involve three basic elements: (1) self-observavation, (2) environmental programming, and (3) behavioral programming. Self-observation, or the process of recording information about oneself, is often referred to as *self-recording* or *self-monitoring*. Environmental programming involves manipulating naturally occurring events that precede, and consequences that follow, a behavior that needs to be changed. An example is offering a child a dollar for moving some bricks and then praising him when he completes the task. Behavioral programming includes self-administered consequences of behavior, such as self-reward or self-punishment. For example, a woman might say to herself, "I'm going to watch soap operas, but not until I finish ironing." This book focuses primarily on the first element in Mahoney and Thoreson's self-control model, namely, self-monitoring. The other two concepts are described to a lesser degree; their purpose is to serve as natural extensions of the self-monitoring process.

Purposes of Self-Monitoring

We have begun our introduction to self-monitoring by discussing one of its practical uses, that is, grocery shopping. Actually, the process can be used in numerous ways to accomplish a variety of objectives. Let us now examine more closely the purposes for which self-monitoring is intended.

Introduction

There are three basic purposes for self-monitoring. These include behavioral assessment, self-regulated behavioral therapy, and use as a preliminary step in a more complex self-management process. A representative schematic might be drawn as follows:

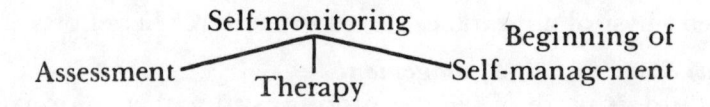

```
                  Self-monitoring
                         |         Beginning of
     Assessment          |         Self-management
                      Therapy
```

Each of these purposes is discussed below in more detail.

Assessment

Teachers and educational diagnosticians are frequently asked to perform a variety of diagnostic procedures. These procedures include a wide range of informal techniques, as well as standardized and criterion-referenced tests. Standardized tests measure the performance of a person who is being compared to others, whereas criterion-referenced tests are used to measure a person's performance against set criteria. Many of the informal procedures and criterion-referenced measures require behavioral counts. Because of the time these counts require when they are done by a teacher or parent, self-monitoring offers an excellent alternative, but only if the child understands the procedure and agrees to cooperate.

When self-monitoring is used for assessment, it is important for the student to be accurate (Kazdin, 1974a). In fact, this is the one purpose of self-monitoring in which accuracy is most crucial.

Collection of data for establishing a baseline is considered a type of assessment. Baseline data are described in Chapter 2 in more detail, but for now it is sufficient to understand that a baseline refers to the frequency of a particular behavior in its natural state.

Therapy

Self-monitoring is often therapeutic in and of itself, without additional reinforcement. When a behavior improves as a result of merely being counted, the change is referred to as *reactivity*. This is discussed in more detail later in the text. Tharp and Wetzel (1969) called this phenomenon the "intervention effect of the baseline period." This change is often temporary, however, unless unprogrammed or unscheduled reinforcers happen to follow the behavior that needs to be changed. For example, an adolescent girl was using self-monitoring to lose weight. While gathering baseline data, her weight began to decline slowly. However, her boyfriend's unexpected comments about her improved physical appearance served to reinforce her efforts.

Initial Stage of Self-Management

A third purpose of self-monitoring is to gather information that can be used in a self-management program. That is, baseline data can be collected to establish individual norms for a given behavior. Then, an intervention strategy can be initiated. Also, a determination can easily be made as to whether a potential reinforcer (or punisher) is having the desired result during the intervention period. At this time, the effects of an intervention are compared to previous counts taken during the baseline period. The basic idea is to analyze the changes that have occurred. This explains the origin of the term *behavior analysis*. For example, one child bit his fingernails an average of seven times a day. When he began to apply a hot substance to his nails, the frequency rate dropped to less than once per week. He concluded that his self-management program was highly effective.

Other Purposes

In addition to these three general purposes, self-monitoring has been successful in teaching a wide variety of behaviors across multiple settings. For example, self-monitoring has been used to improve story writing (Ballard & Glynn, 1975), on-task behavior (Glynn, Thomas, & Shee, 1973), work behaviors of female juvenile offenders (Seymour & Stokes, 1976), hyperactivity (Bornstein & Quevillon, 1976), and study habits (Horner & Brigham, 1979). In addition, the process has been used to ameliorate academic performance (Bailey, 1979) and classroom behavior (O'Leary & Dubey, 1979), assign grades (Davis & Rand, 1980), train parents (Csapo, 1979), and measure job performance (Meyer, 1980).

The process of monitoring one's own behavior may have particular utility in special education. The empirical research in this area has focused primarily on students with learning disabilities (Swanson, 1981) and mental retardation (Horner &

Brigham, 1979). In addition, some attention has been given to students in regular classrooms who exhibit behavior problems (Piersall & Kratochwill, 1979). Relatively little information has been reported with respect to such exceptionalities as sensorily impaired, multihandicapped, gifted, or seriously emotionally disturbed. Some current textbooks on the topic of emotional disturbance offer a general description of self-monitoring but fail to provide empirical data supporting its use with this population. A notable exception is Kauffman (1981).

Regardless of where most researchers have focused their attention, self-monitoring is a viable approach for a wide range of students, including those with handicaps. Type of disability is often of minimal importance. Furthermore, degree of disability is important only in selecting the form of self-monitoring used for counting and recording data. Degree of disability is also a consideration in determining the extent to which a student can accept personal responsibility for his or her self-monitoring program. The key to the use of self-monitoring by all students— whether handicapped or not—is to understand the process and to have sufficient incentive to implement it.

Advantages of Self-Monitoring

There are many advantages to self-monitoring, for both students and teachers. Parents and siblings can benefit, also. Some of the more common advantages are listed below.

Facilitates the Learning of Responsible Behavior

Most individuals acquire some degree of self-monitoring skills for activities of daily living without a planned instructional program. In the process of learning these skills, they receive many social reinforcers in the form of compliments and other types of peer approval, as well as approval from authority figures.

Not everyone is fortunate enough to mature in an environment that offers a wide range of successful experiences and social reinforcement. Some youngsters receive few social rewards and are often described as unreliable, inefficient, and disorganized. Tasks that need to be completed often seem impossible to them. In fact, these students may be at a loss in determining even where to begin in tackling their problems.

In some instances, specially trained teachers are available to work with small classes and make a concerted effort to reach these students. When this is the case, students hopefully can learn the necessary academic and life-support skills to cope successfully. Most of this intervention has historically occurred at the elementary level. As students progress to junior and senior high school, due to the structure of the schools, support has frequently been withdrawn or reduced. In the meantime, the students' responsibilities are gradually increasing. In spite of these problems, some students adapt and learn to complete tasks in an organized, efficient, and reliable manner. Others fail to make this transition and are referred to special programs or drop out of school. The vast majority of problem children learn a limited number of coping strategies and proceed through life succeeding in some tasks and failing in others. Self-monitoring could improve the eventual adjustment of many of these individuals.

Some children behave rather well when they are aware their behavior is being directly observed by an authority figure. Self-monitoring carries this phenomenon a step further by encouraging positive behaviors as an individual observes himself or herself.

Allows Observation of "Hidden" Behaviors

Some behaviors are highly visible and tend to occur in public. That makes them relatively easy for a teacher or parent to observe and record. However, for behaviors that are difficult to observe, self-monitoring may be preferred. This also applies to "hidden" behaviors in the school. For example, time spent between classes, in the lunchroom, at recess, in the bathroom, and before and after school, is time during which students have the most immediate access to their personal behaviors. It is also the time when students frequently encounter the majority of their behavioral problems.

Maximizes Use of Teacher Time

A general problem with gathering observational data involves teacher time. Demands upon teacher time seem to increase every year. Teachers often would like to collect information on individual students but lack sufficient time. Students, when properly trained in self-monitoring procedures, can collect this data, thus saving valuable teacher time.

Time can also be equated to money. Teacher time is expensive. Whenever self-monitoring is used, the time required for behavioral instruction is reduced. This not only saves money but frees the teacher for other instructional duties.

May Improve Self-Awareness

Elementary and junior and senior high students with a history of problems often fail to understand the relationship between their behaviors and the resulting consequences. Self-monitoring is an effective way of addressing this credibility problem since each student records his or her own data. The process thus increases believability and improves the students's role as a member of the behavior-change team.

Self-monitoring encourages an individual to understand the purpose of selected behaviors. He or she may also learn what a change in behavior might mean in terms of short-term (e.g., a hug) or long-term (e.g., increased peer acceptance) benefits.

In addition, students who monitor their own behavior often receive satisfaction from accepting personal responsibility. This responsibility may be one of the few times in their lives they have exerted a high degree of self-initiative. Success in this endeavor may produce increased efforts to gain control over other aspects of their lives.

Allows Generalizations to Other Environments

Self-monitoring has applicability in a variety of environments, including the home, school, and community. Many teachers complain that positive behaviors learned at school do not carry over into the home. The reverse may also be true. Self-monitoring may be useful in this regard, particularly if parents are trained to understand and support the process.

Allows Work on Low-Priority Behaviors

Most of us have undesirable behaviors that are low priority in terms of our desire to correct them. Such behaviors could include sleeping late, watching too much television, overeating, and talking excessively on the telephone. Low-priority behaviors also occur in every classroom, where they include slouching in desks, daydreaming, chewing gum, and reading questionable material. (Naturally, the degree of priority is a matter of personal opinion.) Because of demands resulting from more pressing concerns, low-priority behaviors are rarely addressed. Self-monitoring, however, provides an excellent vehicle for correcting minor problems.

Affords Maximum Use of General Observational Skills

Many skills used in general observation are also applicable to self-monitoring. Some students are excellent observers and even tend to remember minute details without prompting. Despite these skills, self-observation is often not considered, particularly in terms of improving one's own behavior. Students may be surprised to learn that their observational skills can be used in this exciting manner.

Can Be Introduced Early in the Educational Process

Self-monitoring is so simple that it can be successfully taught to children at the kindergarten and first-grade levels (Bates & Bates, 1971). The fact that children can accept responsibility for their own behavior at this age is important. If basic self-monitoring rules can be acquired early, the implications for later adjustment are substantial.

Self-monitoring is an initial step in gaining self-control. Self-monitoring skills can be used throughout a person's life and can be among the most important competencies acquired in school. More specifically, the self-monitoring process can be used to: (1) help students become more responsible, (2) collect data in private or internalized situations, (3) save valuable teacher time, (4) teach the relationship between behavior and its consequences, (5) teach behaviors that can be generalized to a variety of environments, (6) allow improvement of low-priority behaviors, (7) permit maximum use of observational skills, and (8) introduce self-responsibility at an early age. These are but a few examples of what can be accomplished with self-monitoring. After students learn self-monitoring skills, they can even be taught to arrange their personal environment to avoid many problems. They can also enhance the process by providing self-administered consequences in the form of reinforcers and punishers.

Self-Monitoring and Individual Differences

Self-monitoring allows maximum individualization. In fact, no one is more responsible for a student's behavior in the final analysis than himself or herself. Therefore, when training students to use self-monitoring, teachers should acknowledge the effects of individual differences on the outcome. The following summary of individual differences is adapted from a list developed by Karoly and Kanfer (1982):

Introduction

1. Older students are typically better prepared to use self-monitoring than younger children. Young children, however, can use the approach successfully provided that strategies are highly structured and concrete and provided that they receive proper training. More mature children will often be observed inventing new ways to use self-monitoring, as well as altering the process to accommodate unforseen factors.
2. Students are more likely to use self-monitoring successfully when trained by persons of their respective race.
3. Students often practice self-monitoring skills better when a reward is provided. Children from lower economic levels generally respond more favorably to external rewards (e.g., free time, smile, praise). In contrast, middle-class students are apt to be sufficiently motivated by the successful experience itself.
4. Students at all activity levels, including subdued and impulsive ones, can benefit from self-monitoring. More active children, however, may require additional structure and tangible reinforcement.

Common Terms

Several behavioral terms are used frequently throughout this text. In order to encourage maximum understanding, these terms need to be defined in the simplest possible manner:

Target behavior: A behavior that has been selected to change and has been written down in explicit, objective terms. If, for example, a child routinely greets a peer with a derogatory name and a desire exists to change the greeting to a more appropriate one, then the greeting has been targeted.

Self-monitoring (Self-recording; Self-observation): Observing oneself for the purpose of counting, and ultimately improving, target behaviors; this process can also be used for assessment purposes.

Consequences: The events that immediately follow a behavior; they may increase the behavior, decrease the behavior, or be neutral in their effect.

Reinforcer: A *consequence* that increases the probability of the behavior it follows; reading a book of one's choice following completion of seatwork, for example, may lead to an increased rate of seatwork.

Punisher: The presentation of an aversive stimulus or removal of a reinforcer; both actions tend to decrease the likelihood of a behavior. An example is taking away free time by assigning extra homework following disobedience of class rules.

Contingency: The prearranged link between a predetermined behavior and the planned consequences that follow; a *contingency* is usually a reward but may also be a *punisher*. Praise might be contingent upon successful completion of twenty-five push-ups, for example.

Stimulus change: An alteration in the physical surroundings of a person; examples include a light being turned on or off and the noise of an electric fan starting and stopping.

Cue: A stimulus change that makes a person aware that a particular behavior is about to occur or that a specific behavior will be followed by certain consequences; when a teacher begins to call roll, the class knows to get quiet.

Data (singular *datum*): Quantitative behavioral information; the fact that a child bites his fingernails an average of ten times a day is *data*.

Baseline Data: Information that reveals how frequently a behavior occurs on the average; it is often gathered prior to introduction of a management plan. If a child averages talking inappropriately in class twenty-two times a day over a one-week period prior to the teacher's implementing a corrective plan, that frequency is the *baseline*.

Setting: The environment in which behavior occurs, including accompanying activities; examples include being in a classroom, doing a science experiment, or sitting in the home watching television.

Modeling: The process of copying or imitating the behavior of another person such as a little girl dressing like her mother.

Extinction: The reduction of a target behavior following the removal of a *reinforcer* that has previously been maintaining the behavior; an example is a teacher ignoring a child's complaints about getting too much work, and the complaints ceasing.

Generalization: The process of applying in one setting that which is learned in another; for example, a child who learns to write letters to friends can express himself or herself in writing for other purposes as well.

Maintenance: The continuance of a learned behavior over time; a child who continues to count behaviors over time after his or her teacher has taught him or her the basic procedure is *maintaining* the counting behavior.

John was an exceptionally bright high school student who was classified as emotionally disturbed. He also met the criteria for being gifted. His problems included frequent fights and other "blow-ups" during and between classes. Some classmates admired him for "not taking anything from anybody." Other students were afraid of him. This reputation attracted the attention of students trying to prove how tough they were. They often tried to provoke John into a fight and found it easy to do. Usually, John was blamed for the fights, which occurred frequently. In one respect, John probably enjoyed his reputation. The problem was that he was not in control of the situation which was especially frustrating.

John was very articulate, particularly about his problems. He had probably learned to talk about his problems from his special education teachers. He liked most of his teachers and wanted to please those who seemed to have a sincere interest in him. He could also list those long-term problems he might face if he continued in his present behavior pattern. John was selected as a candidate for self-monitoring and became very enthusiastic about it. He reported that he could see improvement and seemed to like the idea of becoming involved in changing his own behavior. He started using the procedure for other problems.

Unfortunately, one of his other problems was losing simple possessions, including textbooks, pencils, paper, and keys. In fact, he really felt bad when he lost several weeks of self-monitoring data. It was at this point that decision was made to introduce reinforcers contingent upon his turning in weekly accumulations of self-monitoring data. These reinforcers included two free tickets to the next varsity football game and permission to use the family car for one night.

Conclusion

Behaviorists are specialized professionals who focus on cause and effect relationships that underlie human behavior. Many of the theories and practices that behaviorists apply to human functions were initially learned from studies involving animals. Behaviorists contend that individuals can be taught to behave in a desired manner by properly manipulating their environment. That is, people respond favorably to events and items they value, and they attempt to avoid unfavorable stimuli. Simply stated, we all live in a world that offers both rewards and punishments. We behave accordingly.

Much of the behavioral literature involves the manipulation of one person's environment by another. For example, a teacher manipulates a student's environment to facilitate learning by rearranging the desks. Similarly, a parent manipulates a child's environment by requiring him to study rather than watch television. This pattern, by definition, includes two or more principal parties. Obviously, not all learning is acquired in this manner. Individuals can also be totally responsible for certain aspects of their own behavior. Self-monitoring provides them with a tool to accomplish this purpose.

Chapter 2

AN OVERVIEW OF THE SELF-MONITORING PROCESS

An individual who uses self-monitoring to improve his or her behavior must have a fundamental understanding of the technology involved. The three basic elements of behavior change are antecedents *(A)*, behavior *(B)*, and consequences *(C)*. They are sometimes called the *ABCs* of behavior. Antecedents refer to events that occur before a particular behavior. For example, a child puts up a sign with a slogan such as "Honesty is the best policy" or "Cleanliness is next to Godliness" as a reminder to behave in a certain way. Consequences refer to the results of a behavior. For example, a child who tells a lie is ignored by his peers, who walk away. Self-monitoring focuses upon the *B*, behavior. In most cases it refers to behavior that is described in observable, easy-to-measure terms. For example, the child in the last example may desire to reduce the frequency of his lying from an average of three times a day to less than once per week. He may count and then record his lies to monitor progress toward his goal.

In this chapter we will discuss each of these *ABC* elements in detail. First, however, it is important to understand the process of operationally defining specific behaviors, as well as to identify various techniques for recording these behaviors.

Operational Definitions of Specific Behaviors

To define a behavior operationally is to state its characteristics in easily observable terms. This is important if an observer has to make a decision as to whether a distinct behavior has indeed occurred.

Behaviors are normally observed in their natural settings. The vast majority of these settings are informal in nature. Despite this informality, the observational process must be precise. The more precise, the more likely it is that the behavior management plan will succeed. Even if the plan is not successful, precision measurement is likely to provide viable feedback to reformulate the plan.

Precision measurement requires that target behaviors be operationally defined. Cartwright and Cartwright (1974) recognized this need when they succinctly stated: "The behavior or event being recorded should be described so specifically that any time a child displays the behavior, it can be easily determined whether or not the behavior has occurred. Some behaviors may prove difficult to describe and, in these instances, a variety of examples which describe instances of the behavior can be given to further specify the descriptions" (p. 52).

Certain verbs are more helpful in writing operational definitions than others. A list of verbs for behaviors that are directly observable is provided below:

to mark	to put on
to underline	to number
to write	to label
to say	to place
to fill in	to cross out
to remove	to circle
to point out	to read orally
to walk	to state
to count orally	to cross out

Other behaviors are not directly observable. A sample list of verbs for these behaviors includes the following:

to develop	to concentrate
to generate	to recognize
to infer	to apply
to apply	to feel
to determine	to think
to discriminate	to appreciate
to solve	to test
to perceive	to create
to learn	to discover
to know	to like
to understand	to experience

Many of these verbs were taken from a larger list initially published by Alberto and Troutman (1982).

Typically, the process of operationally defining behavior begins with a general description or listing of characteristics of a student (e.g., disruptive). This description may originate from the teacher concerned with changing the behavior, or it may be contributed by another teacher. The next step in the process is to examine the observable behaviors that lead to the description of "disruptive." The term *disruptive* may refer to many different descriptions by different teachers. In this example, *disruptive* refers to *problems in interacting with peers in the classroom, during lunch, and between classes.* This latter description is more useful than merely referring to the student as "disruptive;" however, it is still inadequate, since two people attempting to observe and record the described behavior could easily obtain different results. The final step is to state the specific behaviors in even more observable ways.

Let us consider the following examples of appropriate and inappropriate ways for gaining peer attention. Appropriate ways include tapping a peer on the shoulder and using the child's name with volume of voice such that it cannot be heard twenty feet away. Inappropriate behaviors include tapping or hitting with intensity, using derogatory comment, using volume of voice such that it can be heard from twenty feet away, and whistling.

Although the observer is not expected to measure twenty feet with a tape measure, the twenty foot criterion is merely a guideline for the observer's benefit. Teaching students to define their behavior operationally is often easier than might be expected. Students understand hitting, tapping, yelling, and calling names much better than global characteristics such as "disruptive."

Types of Behavioral Recordings

There are several ways a person can record a behavior that he or she desires to change. The most common procedures used for self-monitoring include permanent product recording, event recording, and interval time sampling.

Permanent product recording is used when a behavior results in a lasting record of some type. Examples include worksheets with written answers and written homework assignments. Other examples of permanent products include beds that are made, carburetors that are assembled, and cigarette butts that are smoked. These products allow a teacher or student to calculate and record daily totals on a weekly tally sheet at his or her convenience. This results in a given rate of behavior (e.g., number of cigarettes smoked per day).

Event recording is used when appropriate permanent products are unavailable and the behavior has a concrete beginning and end. An individual counts the number of specific behaviors that occur in a day, a class period, or some other predetermined length of time. Behaviors should occur no more than once every few seconds for this method to be effective. Event recording is very common and is usually converted into such meaningful terms as *words read per minute* or *number of self-initiated conversations per day*. In essence, it is typically stated in a combination of behavior count (e.g., conversations initiated) and an appropriate, consistent recording time unit (e.g., per day, hour, or minute). As with permanent product recording, this method results in a specific rate of behavior.

Interval time sampling is used with behaviors that occur more frequently than once every few seconds or that do not have a clear beginning and end. It is also used when event recording intrudes too much on an individual's time. It is usually less accurate than event recording. An audio cue of some sort, from a cassette recorder to a kitchen timer, may be used to help an individual remember to record the behavior. When the beep or bell is heard, the person simply marks whether the behavior was, or was not, occurring at the instant. The beep or bell can be set for intervals of time from seconds to minutes. The time period typically remains constant. The time interval for the beep or bell is designed to "catch" the behavior occurring. Therefore, if the behavior happens infrequently, a short (thirty-second) interval might be used. If the behavior happens frequently, a longer interval (five minutes) might be preferred.

Despite its advantages, time sampling often tends to over- or underestimate the frequency of a behavior. Another problem with time sampling is its dependence upon an apparatus for cueing (e.g., the buzzer or bell). The approach is usually used when an apparatus is readily available. However, time sampling is sometimes used without an audio cue. The individual merely records whether the behavior is occurring when he or she thinks of it. For example, when a person is on the playground, between classes, or at home, a cueing apparatus may be unavailable or awkward to use. Class time is often the best time to use time sampling because of the structure and availability of a cue. (Note: Some wristwatches have automatic timers that could be used for a cue in a variety of settings.) The result of time-sampling recording is the number or percentage of intervals in which the behavior occurs, as compared to the total number of intervals used. For example, a student might be on task 37 percent of the time when a buzzer sounds.

Self-Evaluation with Self-Recording

Permanent products can be analyzed quantitatively or qualitatively. The number of beds made or the percentage of math problems done correctly can be quantitatively recorded. Also, quality of handwriting can be rated, for instance, on a one-to-five scale, based upon specific criteria. When an individual uses a qualitative measure to evaluate his or her own behavior, the process is referred to as *self-evaluation*.

As stated earlier, data gathered with event recordings are usually stated in terms of the number of responses per consistent unit of time (minute, hour, class period). Also, time-sampling data are usually converted into the number or percentage of intervals in which the behavior occurred at the time of a cue. Both event and time-sampling data can include qualitative measures, thus allowing self-evaluation. For example, a student may count and rate himself or herself on the appropriateness of interactions with peers and adults, based upon set criteria. Totals can be computed for each rating (e.g., number of appropriate interactions and number of inappropriate interactions). As with any kind of evaluation, specific measurement criteria make self-evaluation easier.

Self-Monitoring and Teacher-Monitoring

For each recording technique that we have described, it usually is advisble for both the teacher and the student to be involved in the process as it is being learned. This may seem unusual in discussing self-monitoring, in that the term implies an individual working alone. However, self-monitoring is properly taught as an extension of teacher-monitoring. That is, a specific behavior (e.g., self-monitoring) is often learned best by observing another individual who is demonstrating the skill. In a classroom environment, the "other individual" can be a peer who is already skilled at self-monitoring. Most likely, however, the person is the teacher who is monitoring the student's behavior. As a teacher counts the number of times a student speaks out in class without first raising his or her hand, the student initially observes what the teacher has done. Later, the student can make the counts by himself or herself.

Another option is for the teacher to monitor his or her own behavior, for example, the number of times he or she uses "you know . . ." in a particular class lecture. The information could then be shared with the class or with a particular student.

While learning the process, the teacher and student should independently record selected behaviors to assure that reasonable agreement is achieved and maintained. The level of agreement is called *reliability*. The process is discussed in detail later in the text.

The teacher should use a recording technique before expecting a student to try it. It may also be advisable to check the way a target behavior is defined by trying to record it. A particular recording technique may work fine once a behavior is redefined with more specificity.

In summary, one of the primary responsibilities of a teacher is to demonstrate for the student how to self-monitor. Furthermore, a teacher should allow the student to practice recording specific behaviors until reasonable levels of agreement with an independent recorder (e.g., the teacher or a peer) are achieved. Comparisons are only valid for time periods in which both persons are recording. Although reasonable agreement between the student and independent observers is desirable, self-monitoring can still be effective without it.

Reactivity

There is often a tendency for an individual who is being observed to react by changing his or her behavior. This phenomenon is called *reactivity,* or *reactivity to observation.* When a teacher or other adult monitors a student's specific behavior, the behavior being observed may or may not be among the ones that react or change due to observation. In fact, the altered behavior could appear to have no relationship to the target behavior. For example, a teacher could be observing the ways a student gains peer approval. Reactivity in a disruptive student could result in quiet, more inactive responses.

Degree of reactivity can be affected by several factors. Some of these include how obvious the observation process appears, the student's previous experiences with being observed, and previous consequences that followed observation. When an individual observes his or her own behavior, reactivity is most likely due to the obvious nature of the observation process.

When observation is conducted by someone other than the individual being observed, reactivity typically lasts four or five days. With self-observed behavior, reactivity may last far longer, up to thirty days. Also, the effects of reactivity are usually desirable. That is, the person tends to increase appropriate behaviors and decrease inappropriate ones.

The self-monitoring process itself may induce sufficient change over sufficient time to solve a problem behavior. This is a basic therapeutic advantage of self-monitoring. Because of the importance of reactivity, the concept will be used several times throughout the text.

Conceptualizing the Self-Monitoring Process

We have now discussed (1) operationalizing definitions of target behaviors, (2) types of behavioral recordings, (3) the qualitative aspects of self-evaluation, (4) the role of the teacher as an example in learning self-monitoring, and (5) the meaning of reactivity. This discussion has included the concepts of self-recording and self-evaluation, both of which relate to the *B*, or behavior, component of the *ABCs* of behavior change. A schematic of these concepts looks something like this:

The Behavior Component

| Antecedents Behavior | Behavior | Consequences of Behavior |

Self-Monitoring (S-M)	
Self-Recording	Self-Evaluation
a. Event Recording	a. Permanent Products
b. Time-Sampling Recording	
c. Permanent Product Recording	

The Consequences of Behavior

The consequences of behavior in a self-monitoring program are the events that immediately follow one or more occurrences of the behavior. Much of the learning that occurs in humans is a result of planned and unplanned consequences. Our natural and social environment provides many unplanned consequences of behavior. For example, children discover that touching a hot object results in pain. Further touching of hot objects decreases as a result of this experience. Also, a hungry baby cries and receives milk as a consequence of crying. This naturally increases the frequency of crying. Unplanned consequences of behavior can lead to desirable changes in behavior (e.g., decreased touching of hot objects) or to less desirable changes (e.g., increased crying). In a structured self-monitoring program, the consequences of a behavior are carefully planned to increase or decrease the frequency of a target behavior.

In a self-monitoring program, there are three types of consequences: (1) *reinforcers*, or those that lead to an increase in the behavior; (2) *punishers*, or those that lead to a decrease in the behavior; and (3) *neutral consequences*, or those that have little or no effect on the behavior. Reinforcing, punishing, and neutral consequences vary among individuals, although teachers can use consequences that they speculate will lead to desired increases or decreases in behavior. The record of a behavior's increasing, decreasing, or staying the same over time is the only way of determining whether a consequence is actually reinforcing, punishing, or neutral. This is why the importance of detailed record keeping when using self-monitoring is stressed.

Self-Administered Reinforcers

While the self-monitoring process is being taught, teachers usually administer consequences of behavior. As students observe the process, they learn to provide self-administered consequences for their behavior. For example, they might allow themselves an hour of watching television for completing thirty math homework problems. Preferred activity reinforcers (e.g., watching television) offer several advantages for self-administered and teacher-administered consequences planned to increase behaviors.

Three points are important when selecting reinforcers for self-monitoring. Reinforcers should be typically inexpensive or free, usually available to the individual, and naturally occurring consequences that the individual can take with him or her to a variety of settings.

Tangible items are frequently used with teacher-administered consequences for increasing behavior. This is particularly true for students at the lower end of the motivational spectrum. Coins, candy, toys, and cereal are examples of tangible items that may be used to increase behavior. For students providing self-administered consequences, tangible items may or may not be feasible. Students often have less access or control over, or money to purchase, tangibles than adults. Students may self-administer snacks that their parents already provide or use their allowance to purchase tangibles, contingent upon the nature of their behavior and parent approval.

Verbal and nonverbal consequences are also used by teachers to increase behaviors. Praise, smiles, and pats on the shoulder are examples of planned teacher-administered consequences. Students using self-administered consequences to increase behavior can be taught to praise themselves aloud or silently. This form of self-administered consequences, like the others we have discussed, may or may not lead to an increase in future behavior in a given individual. The proof is in the record of the behavior over time.

Self-Administered Punishers

Teachers frequently administer consequences designed to decrease certain behaviors, such as breaking class rules. A child may be required as a consequence of a behavior to lay his or her head down on the desk for a few minutes, go to the principal's office, sit in a corner, or receive a verbal reprimand. These consequences may or may not lead to a future decrease in the behavior. In a behavior change program, the term *punisher* can only be used when a consequence that follows the behavior leads to a decrease in the behavior. Even then, the punisher and consequence apply only to the given individual. Self-administered punishers are usually self-statements in the form of verbal reprimands. They may also include prearranged penalties in which the student loses money or privileges previously held by a trusted individual (e.g., a parent or older sibling).

Let us consider a student who is trying to reduce the number of times she interrupts the teacher or her peers. She might say to herself each time the behavior occurs, "Oh, darn, I did it again, and that won't help Jane to like me." These self-reprimands can also be used to decrease errors in academic or self-help skills. Another possibility is for the student to agree or contract with a parent to give up a nickel of her allowance for having more than ten interruptions per day.

A consequence is only punishing when it immediately follows the behavior and the record of the behavior shows a decrease over time. Punishers, whether teacher-, parent-, or self-administered, should be used more sparingly than self-administered reinforcers. For example, the student with the contract should be able to earn money when the interruptions go below ten per day. The reason punishers should be used sparingly is that they could conceivably result in a child exhibiting too few appropriate behaviors or becoming shy and withdrawn.

A teacher or parent might reasonably question whether students recording their behavior might cheat when consequence involve money or privileges. A system of bonus points for accuracy is useful with this potential problem.

If we diagrammed the topics covered to this point, our self-monitoring model might look like this:

The Consequences Component

Antecedents of Behavior   Behavior   Consequences of Behavior

Self-Monitoring (S-M)	
Self-Recording	Self-Evaluation
a. Event-Recording	a. Permanent Products
b. Time-Sampling Recording	Self-Administered Reinforcement
c. Permanent Product Recording	Self-Administered Punishment

Self-Administered Antecedents/Self-Instruction

Teachers often provide spoken and written items called *antecedents*. These items are designed to increase or decrease the probability of a behavior before it occurs. Specific antecedents might include posted classroom rules, with the consequnces for breaking them as well. They could also be verbal statements, such as "While I'm out of the room, anyone leaving their seat or talking to their neighbors will stay in at recess" or "Anyone finishing their work before the end of class may play a game quietly." Antecedents are effective because they have been used successfully in the past. Further, students have previously received reinforcers or punishers for their behavior or observed other students that did. Antecedents, by themselves, have no control over behavior, except for the control gained from earlier use and the consequences of behavior encountered or observed. Antecedents are powerless without past or present reinforcers or punishers.

Self-administered antecedents are similar to self-warnings of punishers or self-promises of reinforcers. They can be taught to students by using the following steps (Meichenbaum & Goodman, 1971, p. 32):

1. An adult model performs a task while talking to himself out loud (cognitive feelings).
2. The student performs the same task under the direction of the model's instructions (overt external guidance).
3. The student performs the task while instructing himself aloud (overt self-guidance).
4. The student whispers the instructions to himself as he goes through the task (faded, overt self-guidance).
5. The student performs the task while guiding his performance via private speech (covert self-instruction).

An example of self-instructional training was provided by Bornstein and Quevillon (1976): Scott, who was four years old, was described as "a disciplinary problem because he simply was unable to follow direction for any extended period of time." He often mainfested violent outburst of temper and rarely completed any tasks in the preschool. Rod, also four years old, was considered out of control in the classroom, as manifested by his short attention span, aggressiveness, and general overactivity. Tim, the last four-year-old treated, spent most of his time walking around the room, staring off into space, and/or not attending to tasks or instructions. Bornstein and Quevillon systematically documented these behaviors by conducting classroom observations.

Using the self-instructional training of cognitive modeling, followed by overt and covert rehearsal, the children were taught to use the following self-verbalizations: (1) questions about the task (e.g., "What does the teacher want me to do?"); (2) answers to questions in the form of cognitive rehearsal (e.g., "Oh, that's right; I'm supposed to copy that picture"); (3) self-instructions to guide the subject through the task (e.g., "O.K., first I draw a line here . . ."); and (4) self-reinforcement (e.g., "How about that? I really did that one well") (pp. 45–46).

Self-instruction is used when a student is having a specific learning problem such as not completing homework assignments. The teacher initially tells the student in detail what must be done to complete assigned tasks. Then, the student repeats the steps to himself or herself just before performing them. Assigned steps might be to (1) select the proper time to begin work, (2) retreat to a quite place, (3) attend to personal needs before beginning, (4) review the work in a general sense, (5) have all resources readily available, and (6) identify a reward for task completion (e.g., a favorite television show or a call to a friend).

The teacher, in order to assist students with self-instruction, must be able to analyze a skill by dividing it into a set of subskills. These subskills must be listed, and then learned, in the proper sequence. Steps are recited for the student by the teacher. The student later says them to himself or herself as an aid in learning. Mastery of subskills will eventually result in learning the larger skills.

We have now added the antecedent component to our self-monitoring diagram.

The Antecedent Component

Antecedents of Behavior • Behavior • Consequences of Behavior

Self-Monitoring (S-M)	
Self-Recording	Self-Evaluation
a. Event Recording	a. Ratings Based upon set criteria
b. Time-Sampling Recording	b. Leading to sub-totals for each rating
c. Permanent Product Recording	c. Using permanent products or event or time-sampling recording

Self-Statements
Self-Promises
Self-Warnings

Self-Administered Reinforcers
Self-Administered Punishers

Conclusion

In this chapter we have reviewed the basic principles that comprise the self-monitoring process. We have discussed the *ABC*s of behavior change, including the behavior itself, its consequences, and its antecedents. We have also described various aspects of self-monitoring that are important if the procedure is to be successful. These aspects include proper definition of target behaviors, types of behavioral recordings, the qualitative nature of self-evaluation, and the role of teacher-monitoring as a model for students who are learning the process.

No matter how well a procedure is conceptualized, it must also be practiced if optimum learning is to occur. This applies to self-monitoring as well as other skills (e.g., shooting a basketball or driving a car). In order to routinely practice self-monitoring, it is essential to have a thorough understanding of its most common elements, that is, counting and recording behaviors. These elements are described in detail in the next chapter.

Chapter 3

COUNTING AND RECORDING TARGET BEHAVIORS

Self-monitoring requires a systematic approach to counting and recording one's own behavior. The extent to which this data collection is taken seriously by the individual often has a significant impact on the strategy's success. The purpose of this chapter is to discuss various considerations that affect data collection. The chapter is divided into four basic sections. These include identification of target behaviors, counting devices and recording mechanisms, helpful hints for counting and recording behaviors, and common problems and possible solutions.

The simplicity of self-monitoring, when it is used properly, contributes to its popularity. For example, proficiency in actually making behavioral counts and recording tabulations need not depend upon the development of highly technical skills or elaborate recording devices. In fact, a review of the research on self-monitoring reveals that the most common recording technique is for students to make tally marks on three-inch by five-inch note cards taped on their desks or near their work areas. This chapter will focus on the ease with which behaviors can be defined, counted, recorded, and improved.

Identification of Target Behaviors

A target behavior is one for which an individual desires a change. The decision that a change is needed may be made by the individual or by others who interact with the person (e.g., teacher, friend, parent). The term *target* is used to describe the behavior because an intervention strategy is "aimed" at it.

Selecting an appropriate target behavior with which to use self-monitoring may or may not present a problem, depending on the individual. Some children have so many problems that it is difficult to focus on one. Other children's problems may be diffuse (e.g., poor attitude, poor parent relations) and thus difficult to define precisely in behavioral terms. Still others may not admit to problems of sufficient magnitude to justify the use of self-monitoring. The remainder may easily identify a major concern. Even with this latter group, it may be necessary to redefine the problem in measurable terms, restate the problem in a more positive sense, or encourage the child to identify a different or alternative target behavior, before self-monitoring can be applied.

The teacher can often play a key role in helping a child identify a target behavior. He or she may already be integrally familiar with the child and may also be able to discuss the child's behavior with parents. In addition, a teacher can reflect on a child's ideas in a type of informal brainstorming session.

Identifying an appropriate target behavior is an important process for two reasons: The child may be in serious need of help in a problem area, and the child may need to practice the skill of identifying target behaviors as part of a self-monitoring training program. When first learning to use self-monitoring, it is important to select a target behavior that is quantifiable, that can be measurably improved with reasonable effort, that the child would like to improve, and that is easily observed.

One of the simplist and most effective methods for identifying a target behavior is to ask the child. This can be done verbally or with a questionnaire. Whatever the method, it is usually advisable to assure privacy and sometimes anonymity. Children do not normally need to know in-depth information about each other's problems, unless for some reason it is advantageous to inform them (e.g., to encourage peers to provide verbal praise).

Questionnaires can also be useful. They usually work best when simply stated, asking only that a child list his or her most inappropriate behavior(s). If more than one behavior is listed, they can be ranked in order of importance. With younger students, a checklist is often helpful; that is, several (e.g., ten) inappropriate behaviors are listed, and the child is then read the list of behaviors and asked which he or she would most like to improve. An open-ended question could be placed at the bottom of the page for the child to mention any behavior not listed.

Another idea for generating possible target behaviors is to supply a written list of open-ended responses. Examples include "I wish . . .," "My biggest problem at home is . . .," "My biggest problem at school is . . .," "I get mad when. . .," and "If I could change anything, I would . . .." Again, privacy should be respected if children are to be honest in their responses.

With children who are reluctant to identify their problems in writing, an interview approach might be helpful. An interview is normally held in private, and includes only the teacher and child. The teacher assumes a leadership role and directs the questioning. When an interview is used, it is important for good rapport to exist between teacher and child. More than one session may be needed before good rapport is established. If a teacher is not successful with an interview approach, and other ideas are futile as well, the school counselor and/or parent may need to become involved.

When conducting an interview, the teacher should make as many mental notes as possible. They should be recorded in writing immediately after a session is completed. Taking notes during a session may make some children uncomfortable.

The teacher should also plan an interview as completely as possible. During the planning stage, it is important to consider a child's personal interests and behavioral history. Talking with other teachers, parents, and the counselor may be helpful. Before involving parents, however, it may be advisable to solicit the student's opinion.

Another idea is to ask students to write an autobiography. Adapted versions of this assignment are to write a family history or to do an eassay entitled "How I Cope with Personal Problems."

Whether a student is actively involved in selecting the target behavior or not, a precise operational definition of the behavior is important. The student may play a key role in writing operational definitions, particularly in suggesting examples of the behavior and describing the setting in which it occurs.

Counting Devices and Recording Mechanisms

The frequency of target behaviors needs to be recorded if self-monitoring is to function effectively. Accuracy is also important but not necessarily critical. Being precise is important when behaviors are recorded for assessment purposes

The basic problem that impedes most people in their efforts to record behaviors is lack of a systematic approach. Simply stated, too much data are often left to memory. This is a primary reason self-monitoring without systematic recording fails. In other instances, target behaviors are too ambiguous (i.e., not operationally defined), and the person is not certain when counting is warranted. Other problems associated with recording behaviors are described in detail in this chapter.

This section is devoted to identifying various ways that students can record target behaviors. For example, how can students make sure they record the number of times they raise their hand in class before asking a question or making a comment? To be reasonably efficient in counting behaviors, a student must have a systematic plan and be conscientious in implementing it. Furthermore, counts must be recorded as soon after the behavior occurs as possible. Otherwise, it is easy to forget that a behavior occurred, the situation in which it was observed, and the consequences that followed.

The precise method for recording behaviors can differ depending on individual preferences and the nature of each response. Before identifying specific procedures, it is important to distinguish between merely counting behaviors and actually providing a lasting record of the count. For example, the number of times a child completes classwork in the alloted time can be counted on a wrist counter and then recorded at the end of the day on a tally sheet or graph. Another example is provided by a student with a weight problem: A simple bathroom scale is ideal for counting pounds, but a record of daily weight must also be maintained. From these examples, it is obvious that data collection can be two separate tasks; counting and recording. In many cases the counting and recording process can be combined. This occurs when an individual places a mark on a notecard after each occurrence of a behavior (e.g., talk-outs in class).

The following chart illustrates some common techniques for counting and recording behaviors. The reader is encouraged to suggest additional items for the list. For further information on counting and recording data, the reader is referred to Ciminero,

Nelson, and Lipinski (1977). This article is a particularly good resource for information about timing devices and electronic equipment.

Table 3-1
COUNTING DEVICES

Simplistic

1. Making tally marks or placing stars on chart or card
2. Transferring common items from one location to another (e.g., paper clips, pennies, or marbles from one pocket to another)
3. Adding beads to a string
4. Placing rings on a peg, preferably color coded
5. Using a pegboard
6. Using a ruler or yardstick

Mechanical

1. Golf stroke counter (Hannum, Thoreson, & Hubbard, 1974)
2. Wrist counters, or variations
   a. Knit Talley (Sheehan & Casey, 1974)
   b. Response Counter (Ciminero, Nelson, & Lipinski, 1977)
   c. Ristkountr (bracelet abacus)(Mahoney, 1974)
3. Weight scales

Timing

1. Wrist watch
2. Alarm clock
3. Stopwatch
4. Kitchen timer
5. Metronome

Electronic

1. Videotape
2. Audiotape
3. Special devices
   a. Cigarette case opener (Azrin & Powell, 1968)
   b. Posture aparatus (Azrin, Rubin, O'Brien, Ayllon, & Roll, 1968)
   c. Gravity-sensitive watch (Schulmann & Reisman, 1959)
4. Telephone recorder

Recording Mechanisms

1. Three by five notecards
2. Checksheet
3. Rating scale
4. Anecdotal records

Table 3-1 continued

---

5. Behavioral menu
6. Behavioral diary
7. Microcomputers
8. Bar graphs, preferably color coded
9. Horizontal/vertical graphs (color coded)(Mahoney & Thoreson, 1974)
10. Countoon (pictoral sequence)(Kunzelman, 1970)

Helpful Hints for Collecting Data

Counting and recording target behaviors are the most basic elements in the self-monitoring process. Learning to execute these skills in an efficient and reliable manner is important. Helpful hints, such as those discussed in this section, should make the task a lot easier.

The counting and recording system should be either portable or highly accessible to the student in the area in which recording is to occur. For example, a wrist counter is portable, while a checksheet on a student's desk is accessible. A person typically needs to have the system in his or her possession (or nearby) at the time a target behavior occurs. Without a convenient system, a person often has to rely on memory. Most of us do not function very effectively if we have to depend entirely on memory.

A counting and recording system should be easy and as practical to use as possible. For example, swapping paper clips from one pants pocket to another to count out-of-state behaviors is fairly simple. The same is true of recording tally marks following each occurrence of a behavior. Conversely, it would be highly impractical for a child to count behaviors by interrupting the teacher to tell him or her each time a response occurs.

Records should be written or at least permanent. For example, an audio- or videotape player preserves records indefinitely. Additionally, counts can easily be verified from these sources. Without a permanent record, we must again depend on memory.

Graphs are excellent visual aids when viewing a progression of behavioral tallies. A bar graph, for example, often means more to a person than a simple number. Color-coded bar graphs may also be a good idea. For example, baseline data could be in blue, and intervention periods in red. Comparisons in progress can then be quickly noted, even by an untrained eye.

A related idea is to display graphs in the classroom. The idea is to stimulate peer pressure. Naturally, displays would be inappropriate if target behaviors were private or personal (e.g., toilet training, bed wetting).

Personalities must also be considered before using a public display of baseline data. Children who are highly introverted or who have a history of related failures might have their feelings easily hurt. Teachers should be sensitive to these possibilities.

Microcomputers are especially useful for creating bar graphs. Software programs can be written or purchased that even applaud when a positive behavioral change occurs. For example, a gifted high school student wanted to use self-monitoring to increase the efficiency of completing homework assignments. He programmed a microcomputer to plot his baseline behavior in a color-coded format. He used blue bars to indicate daily time spent on English, green bars to indicate daily time spent completing mathematics assignments, and red bars to indicate daily time spent on other topics. In this manner he could easily see to what the majority of his time was being devoted. He was also able to establish a reliable baseline to use for comparative purposes once he implemented a reinforcement system.

Counting and recording procedures should be well defined for young children. The more concrete they are, the better. For example, placing pegs in a pegboard each time a child makes 100 percent on a daily spelling test is a concrete activity. Mature students can often handle more abstract responsibilities. For example, they could be expected eventually to record instances of several types of behavior and turn them in at the end of the week.

A simple reward system is often helpful to encourage students to be consistent and accurate when counting and recording. This is particularly important during the training period when children are initially learning the system, or when rewards or punishments depend on accuracy. Also, capable students should have some influence on selection of target behaviors. Rewards can be social in nature (e.g., praise, a pat on the back), or they can be tangible (e.g., a new pencil, fifteen minutes with an educational game).

It might be a good idea to use an incentive system that provides rewards for accurate counts and imposes penalties for inefficient ones. For example, a child could earn five points for each acceptable daily performance, with a bonus of two points for each day recorded within one behavior of the teacher's count. Conversely, each day beyond a one-count margin could penalize the child two points. At the end of the baseline period, the child could use points to purchase predefined privileges (e.g., trip to the library, extra dessert, free time).

Target behaviors should be operationally defined as precisely as possible before beginning to count and record time. For example, is a behavior to be counted each time it occurs at all? Does it have to last a certain length of time? Does it have to reach a certain intensity level? What dimensions of behavior are to be considered? Sulzer-Azaroff, and Mayer (1977) list *topography, intensity, duration, frequency,* and *accuracy* as dimensions. *Latency* could be added to this list.

Let us consider what each of these dimensions means in a classroom setting. If a young girl decides she wants to decrease her out-of-seat behaviors, does standing in her desk to look out of the window qualify as out of seat? What about leaving the desk partially while continuing to touch its top with one hand? This is a question of topography of the behavior, or how it appears or sounds. What if she leaves the desk for ten minutes? This is an example of duration, or how long the behavior occurs. Should being away from the desk for excessive periods count more? If a student is counting the number of derogatory remarks made to teachers, should the remarks be counted only if the teacher can hear them from his or her desk? This is a question of intensity. A student may need to count the number of times he or she shoves or hits his or her peers. Does any form of touching count? The difference between hitting and touching is a matter of intensity. A hit or shove may require that the student receiving the hit or shove be physically moved by the action, whereas touching would not produce this result. A shy student may want to count the number of times she responds verbally when other students initiate conversations. How long does she have in which to respond after a student speaks (e.g., five, ten, twenty seconds)? This is an example of latency.

Topography is always included in an operational definition. Intensity, duration, and latency are important with some behaviors. One of these is usually added to topography in most self-monitoring programs. Frequency and accuracy are more important in recording daily totals than they are in counting behavior. Frequency is the number of responses counted divided by units of time spent recording (responses counted/time spent counting). Accuracy is also stated in percentage form. It is achieved by dividing the number of correct responses by the total number of responses (correct responses/total responses).

It is important to make decisions about satisfactory levels of accuracy before counting actually begins, although adjustments may be made if necessary. Otherwise, baseline data are likely to be misleading. Without reasonable expectations, a child may even experience stress and become disillusioned before beginning.

In the out-of-seat example cited, one possible resolution to the problem is for the girl to use a stopwatch to record the total number of minutes in which she has no physical contact with the desk. Total number of minutes, in this case, is more appropriate for comparison purposes than total number of events. The reverse may be true for the student interested in her verbal responses to other students' initiated conversations.

Another example of variations in how to count behaviors is provided by a young man who desires to lose weight. Should he keep track of the amount and number of each of the kinds of foods he eats? This sort of tabulation often gets confusing. Results are also difficult to compare. It might be more practical if he would simply record his daily weight each morning using bathroom scales.

Some behaviors are easier to count than others. Numerical tabulations that are simple to quantify should be selected. Common examples include number of nails bitten, minutes on the telephone, letters written, hours studying, cigarettes smoked, and pounds lost. In contrast, other interests are difficult to quantify. These include number of friends, amount of time in good humor, and variety of poor social responses from others. There is simply too much personal judgment involved. The same interests, however, can be stated in operational terms (e.g., number of invitations to participate in a social activity).

When gathering baseline data, it is usually advisable to make a note of unusual situations and highly unpredictable behavior counts. For example, an adolescent girl may be attempting to count the number of times she is asked for a date. Her baseline count is likely to be unusual if she counts the week of her junior/senior prom. A note explaining the unusual circumstances may be helpful in understanding the fluctuation.

Another example might involve a boy who wants to decrease the amount of time he spends watching television. If he records data during a holiday break, he is not likely to get a typical measure. Again, a note with a brief description of the circumstances is helpful.

Graphs are especially useful for identifying behavioral patterns. A typical graph might look like Figure 3-1. What might have happened on day six? Perhaps the child was experiencing undue stress resulting from a major test. When an extremely rare event is the reason for this type of fluctuation, it might be advisable to either omit the data or place a note on the graph explaining the circumstances.

Graphs are also useful for illustrating when a baseline behavior has stabilized to the point that an intervention program can begin. In fact, baseline data should continue to be collected until the data stabilize. This usually requires a minimum of one week and may take as long as two to three weeks. Wider ranges may even occur. Extreme variations noted during the first week are usually indications that more time is needed. The level of consistency required for stabilization is often dictated by the nature of the behavior. For example, a healthy person's average daily weight is usually stable. However, the number of times a child engages in physical aggression may vary substantially. Figures 3-2 and 3-3 illustrate this phenomenon.

A determination that stabilization has occurred is usually made by an individual who has had some experience with data collection. The decision is sometimes difficult and subjective, but it becomes easier with time.

Sometimes stabilization never appears to occur. Extreme swings continue even after several weeks have passed. When this happens, it is important to try to identify the cause of the

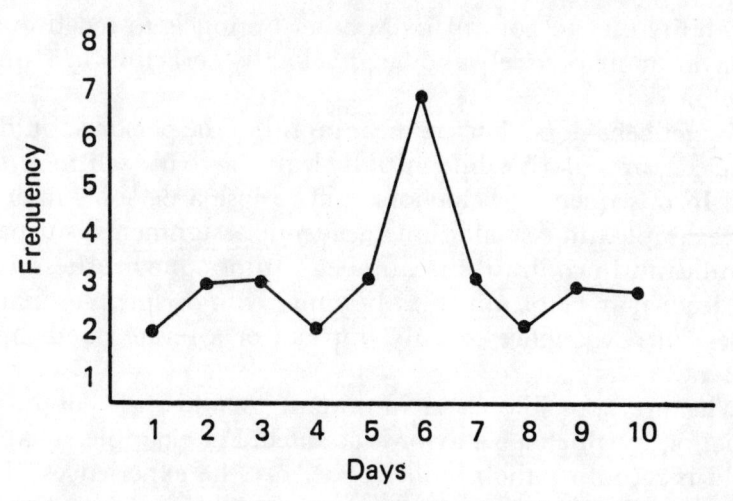

Behavior: Occurrence of a nervous twitch in the right eye.

Figure 3-1

Daily Weight

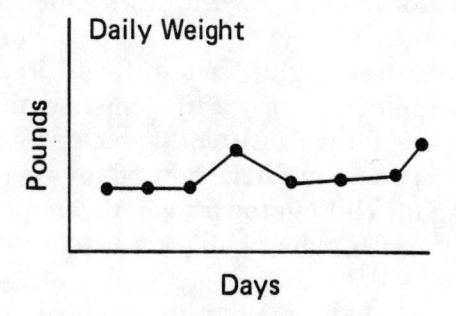

Figure 3-2

Aggressive Behavior

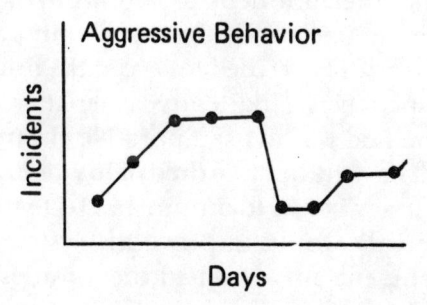

Figure 3-3

instability and to control it. Another option is to redefine the behavior more precisely and begin a totally new effort to acquire baseline data.

Target behaviors that are meaningful to the person should be selected, particularly while initially learning to use self-monitoring. Inconsequential behaviors tend to lose a person's interest. For example, time spent doing academic assignments is usually significant. In contrast, the number of times one brushes his or her teeth may be of minor importance to most people, that is, unless the experience is truly unusual or a severe handicap is present.

Whenever possible, it is important to be consistent in the situation in which a behavior is counted. For example, what if a child is recording the number of seizures he experiences? This may be a difficult or, in some cases, an impossible situation for self-monitoring due to the effects of a seizure upon the individual. (This example provides evidence of how important the physical or social situation can be.) Seizures are often triggered by a particular stimulus in the environment. Common "triggers" include stress, flashing lights, certain foods, loud sounds, fear, and motion. In some children, the trigger is hard to identify, if one exists at all. By recording consistently over a period of time when seizures occur, a pattern might be noticed. By altering the pattern or desensitizing the child to the trigger, the frequency of seizures might be significantly reduced. In some instances, they may even be eliminated.

Time limits should be used to improve counting skills. Counting behaviors over an entire day may be too exhausting. The most common technique is to count only at predesignated times. For example, one student wanted to improve his on-task classroom behaviors. He decided to record the number of minutes per day that he spent being inattentive when there was work to do. His counting method was to use a portable electronic stopwatch. After a couple of days he became tired of his monotonous routine. Interest and accuracy began to diminish. His teacher decided that small time intervals would improve his system. With the new approach, the student only counted the minutes he was off-task during four fifteen-minute periods. These periods were predetermined by the teacher and brought to the student's attention at the end of each fifteen-minute time segment. The student then tabulated the amount of time during the period in which he was off-task (e.g., five minutes). If work was not assigned at the time (e.g., during an assembly), he simply omitted the count.

Providing structure is important when implementing a counting and recording process. Often, it is necessary or advisable to alter the process. This most frequently occurs during the baseline phase. For example, an elementary student may be trying to use a behavioral diary but experiencing difficulty with subjectivity and self-expression. A simple checksheet may need to be substituted. Similarly, a child who frequently loses a checksheet may need to have it taped to his or her desk.

An increase of desirable behaviors should be emphasized rather than a decrease of negative ones. While this suggestion is not always possible, depending on the behavior, it is generally a good rule. For example, let us consider a child who wants to complete more assignments. This student should typically be advised to count the number of completed assignments rather than those not completed.

Behavior counting and recording need to be done consistently, especially during the baseline period. For most people, this practice is not a habit. Few of us practice counting personal behaviors unless there is a need. For self-monitoring to be highly effective, counting needs to become second nature. A good idea to encourage consistency is to pair the counting and recording process with some other daily or regular occurrence. These occurrences might include combing hair, brushing teeth, sitting down to eat, or getting in a car. For example, one child wanted to monitor his daily number of push-ups. His counting was fine, but he usually forgot to record the total. Therefore he decided to do the push-ups immediately before breakfast. Then, before sitting down to eat, he was reminded to record the total.

When initially teaching the counting and recording process, it is often useful to begin with simple techniques and behaviors. The teacher can then proceed to more difficult ones as the children become increasingly familiar with their responsibilities. For example, a beginning target behavior for a first grader might be to come to class with pencil and paper. Once this skill is mastered, the student could advance to including other common items (e.g., crayons, lunch box, reader).

Self-monitoring is truly an individualized process. Children often want to work on diverse assortments of behaviors that are personally meaningful to them. The system allows this luxury and is designed for maximum flexibility.

A teacher's attitude toward self-monitoring is often important to children. Therefore, it may be useful for teachers to introduce the self-monitoring process by describing a personal experience. For example, one teacher told her class about using self-monitoring to encourage herself to do a better job preparing meals for her family. When children are convinced a respected role model likes the system, they are often more inclined to try it themselves. For more mature students, examples of several well-known authors (e.g., Hemingway) who used self-monitoring are provided in the chapter on academic skills.

The self-monitoring process should normally be taught early in the day, when children are fresh and alert. A creative elementary teacher might develop a reading lesson about self-monitoring or possibly even design a self-monitoring game. Short but frequent lessons about self-monitoring are preferred over longer ones.

The simplicity of self-monitoring is sometimes lost when the process is explained to an entire class simultaneously. A better idea is to teach the concept to a small group of one to three students. Their attention and willingness to ask questions is usually better. Children who learn to use the system can also assist in teaching their peers. First-person accounts of self-monitoring experiences are especially useful.

Other important hints to remember when teaching self-monitoring include: (1) the importance of repetition, patience, and having fun; (2) the need to use real-life behaviors that children know and understand; (3) the fact that behaviors are normally acquired in a predictable developmental sequence; (4) the idea that task analysis can be useful in the self-monitoring process; (5) the value to the child of regular feedback from the teacher concerning progress (or lack of progress); (6) the possibil-

Counting and Recording Target Behaviors

ity of applying self-monitoring skills across a wide variety of behaviors; (7) the need to relate self-monitoring, especially during the training period, to behaviors with which the child is familiar; and (8) the need to recognize and appreciate the student as the most important person in the self-monitoring process.

Common Problems and Possible Solutions

Counting and recording behaviors can be very simple (e.g., counting the number of times a child sneezes in a one-hour period for three days and recording the result on a checksheet), or it can be reasonably complex (e.g., counting the number of adverse social reactions by one's peers over a one-month period and recording the daily totals on a microcomputer's color-coded bar graph). That is, the task can be as simple or as complex as it is designed to be. Regardless of the behavior to be monitored, there is no substitute for common sense in setting up a self-monitoring system. However, experience indicates that there are certain aspects of the process that tend to be more problematic than others.

When gathering baseline data, there is a natural tendency to enter the intervention stage as soon as possible. In essence, a child will say to himself or herself, "Why should I fool around with counting behaviors, when I can begin to be rewarded immediately?" In addition to the possibility of a reward, some children are encouraged by a noticeable change in their behavior during the baseline period. They, too, often want to progress immediately to the intervention stage. Patience is important here, as a reliable baseline is essential for making long-term comparisons.

A related problem occurs when children alter their behavior during the baseline stage due to reactivity. This phenomenon is discussed in Chapter 2.

Another frequent problem is lack of a practical coding system when recording behaviors. A simple tally sheet might work fine for some behaviors. The concept becomes more complicated when a child needs to add situational or time-related information. For example, John set up the following coding system to record his fingernail biting:

Setting

    when studying   S
    when TV viewing   T
    when in a nervous social
        situation   N
    when in bed alone   B
    other times   O

His results for the first three days looked like this:

	AM	PM
Day 1	SNN	BOBBOSSS
Day 2	SSSNT	SOBTTTB
Day 3	TSSN	TOSSBTOS

His final summary followed this format (AM/PM):

	Mon.	Tues.	Wed.
S	1/3	3/1	2/3
T	0/0	1/3	1/2
N	2/0	1/0	1/0
B	0/3	1/0	0/1
O	0/2	0/1	0/1
Daily Totals	2/8	6/5	4/7

Three-Day Total: 12/20

Data should be counted and recorded as soon after events occur as possible. If the system is not portable and/or permanent, this process often breaks down. Memory is rarely efficient. Being wrong when trying to recollect behaviors from memory is even worse than not remembering at all. Without an "immediate" system, it is also easy to omit counting altogether. The problem is that many people deal with the emotion of the moment and think they can record information later, when they are more relaxed and have more time.

Some children tend to "hedge" a little when counting behaviors. Their purpose may be to cast themselves in a particularly good or bad light. Children should be warned that this type of cheating tends to diminish the intent of self-monitoring and that they are only fooling themselves, not the system for which they are personally responsible.

Most untrained people, including those at all ages and developmental levels, are not efficient observers. For example, only a small percentage of people can tell you which numerical digits appear on the face of their wrist watch. Observation is an important element in the self-monitoring process. Because of this frequently deficient skill, it is advisable to use some activities during the self-monitoring training period that focus on observation.

Lack of well-defined, easy-to-measure target behaviors is often cited as a problem. Let us consider, for example, a high school athlete who wants to quantify his drinking problem for a self-monitoring program. Should he count the number of ounces of alcohol consumed per day over a two-week period, the number of drinks consumed over this period, or the number of minutes spent in social situations in which he drinks? In most instances, the first choice is preferred because it is the most quantifiable and easy to use for comparison purposes once intervention begins.

When target behaviors are too complex to be easily counted and recorded, it is usually advisable to redefine them in simpler terms. For example, a target behavior such as *reading habits* could be operationally redefined as *number of minutes per day spent reading out of class*, or even *number of pages read per day out of class*. A better defined and more restrictive time period might also be used. Whenever a behavior is redefined, it is customary to begin a totally new baseline period.

Poor baseline data are a primary reason self-monitoring fails (Watson & Tharp, 1972). This problem often relates to poorly defined target behaviors, lack of a portable recording system, or lack of interest in the system. It might also be attributed to an assortment of other problems described in this section.

Incidentally, there are three occasions when it is not necessarily important to record baseline data. The first is when the behavior has never occurred before: There is simply no track record to observe. An example of this situation might be a child's having no passing grades in a particular class. This phenomenon can sometimes be handled by redefining the target behavior. For example, a child may complain that he or she cannot count studying time because he or she never studies. An alternative would be to count the number of opportunities in which studying could occur, as well as the number of times it does occur.

The second occasion is when a target behavior is potentially dangerous to the person, to others, or to property. For example, a juvenile delinquent should not be allowed to count the number of times he or she pulls a knife on someone, and an arsonist should not be counting the number of fires he or she starts. In these cases, it is clearly better to begin with the intervention stage immediately.

The third instance is when a natural event exists that is truly reinforcing and available only temporarily: For example, a high school student is offered a college scholarship with the understanding that he or she must make the honor role during the last academic period. The key is to recognize just how reinforcing the event is. It would be difficult to convince a highly motivated student of the need for collecting baseline data.

Many people who engage in self-monitoring get confused about counting baseline behaviors that occur primarily during peak periods. Examples include a teenage girl monitoring her stressful reactions during exam week and a boy recording spending habits for the two-week period before Christmas. In these instances, the person is not ordinarily concerned with the target behavior, except at the time it poses a problem. There are two ways to cope with this: The first is to be prepared in advance to gather data during peak incidence periods. The other is to practice recording during a simulated experience in preparation for the peak period. Both methods can also be used concurrently.

Failure to recognize a rare behavior often results in a baseline problem. For example, an adolescent girl was displeased with herself about a temper outburst with her mother. She decided to work on this behavior with self-monitoring. The immediate problem was rarity of the behavior. She only lost her temper on infrequent occasions. This phenomenon can be easily observed on a graph. She resolved her problem by omitting baseline altogether, and rewarding herself for the number of days she had only favorable interactions with her mother.

Problems relating to reliability checks are relatively common. As mentioned earlier, reliability is determined by having two or more independent observers, such as the child and the teacher or the child and a peer, count the same behavior. At the end of the predesigned time period, the higher count is divided into the lower count. The result is a reliability coefficient. Any number above .80 is normally considered acceptable.

Reliability is often reduced when behaviors are poorly defined. Reliability is also sometimes impossible to calculate when a target behavior is affective, that is, related to moods or feelings. The reason is that the child may be aware of his or her own affect, but the behavior may not be observable to the second party. Arguments can often be quickly resolved when records are accurately kept and situations well described. It may also be useful to use a third observer as an informal referee or to record behaviors with an audio- or videotape player.

Some behaviors are rather awkward to count or may even be embarrassing. Examples include the number of belches that occur in class and the number of times one is late to class. In these instances, it is sometimes preferable to record the behavior in private, redefine the target behavior, ask a close friend to do the counting, or record the behavior on tape and monitor it later, when alone.

Sometimes a teacher and student will disagree over such topics as the best way to define a target behavior, the target behavior that deserves top priority, the best counting and recording system, the preferred reinforcement, and/or the reinforcement schedule. These items are often negotiable, and the "winner" should be determined on an individual basis. However, "trade-offs" are common. For example, one child decided to go along with the teacher's choice of reward in return for permission to work on the target behavior of his choice.

Because self-monitoring is often therapeutic by itself, there is a natural inclination to depend too heavily on the reinforcing value of improvements in the target behavior. That is, satisfaction resulting from improvement in a target behavior during the baseline period is a type of reward. This reactive value should not be neglected. However, the reinforcement to follow during the intervention stage is important as well. When a child resolves to read more books during leisure time, for example, merely reading a good book may provide a certain amount of reinforcement. However, even though improvement in reading behavior may be noted, there may be even better results when the child begins to receive an external reward (e.g., tickets to a movie) during the intervention stage.

The use of timing devices and electronic equipment often presents unique counting and recording problems. For example, an electronic timer is set to ring at predetermined times during the day. These times are known in advance only by the teacher or by a peer who sets the timer. By chance, a student could be unfairly rewarded even if the positive target behavior is occurring infrequently. It depends on what the child is doing at the time the bell rings. By the same token, unwarranted penalties could also be imposed. That is, the child could be performing admirably, stop to rest, and then have the bell ring. To reduce the problem, the bell could be set to ring often enough to accommodate irregularities.

Even when target behaviors improve to the desired extent, it is sometimes difficult to maintain them over extended periods. The goal of the child who wanted to increase the time spent on leisure reading was to read two additional leisure books per week. She maintained her goal for three months but then began an advanced mathematics class. Her time was then being necessarily devoted to a new topic. In this instance, there was not a problem at all: Her priorities were merely rearranged. However, a boy whose target behavior was to increase study behavior and eliminate cheating was successful for two months, but then he stopped studying and failed two consecutive tests. The cheating resumed. The problem was that reinforcement from higher grades was stronger than the contingency used during self-monitoring. Every case must be analyzed separately when failure to maintain desired behavior presents a problem.

Some students who use self-monitoring tend to have problems of structure when counting and recording behaviors. That is, they fail to adjust when the system develops "bugs." It is essential to know when to be flexible and alter the process as needed and when to continue. That is a special problem for individuals using the process for the first time.

Conclusion

The purpose of this chapter has been to identify and discuss various considerations relating to counting and recording behaviors. While ideas presented might appear relatively simple in several respects, there are numerous cautions that need to be observed. Even the best self-monitoring systems may need to be reevaluated and restructured. For self-monitoring to work with maximum effectiveness, it is important for individuals to accept seriously their responsibilities and to follow the guidelines described.

The first three chapters of this book aimed at preparing students to use self-monitoring with daily behaviors. Our discussions have applied to students of all ages and developmental levels. Naturally, more talented and skilled students will probably be able to use the process with less extensive training than their slower peers. However, even the slowest students should eventually learn enough about self-monitoring to benefit from participation.

All concepts presented thus far apply to both handicapped and nonhandicapped populations, but there are some special considerations that apply to students with handicaps. In the next chapter, we will discuss some of these factors.

Chapter 4

SPECIAL IMPLICATIONS FOR EXCEPTIONAL STUDENTS

Self-monitoring has special applicability for improving behaviors of exceptional children and youth, including the gifted and talented. In this chapter we will discuss self-monitoring's implications for each of the major areas of exceptionality. While the chapter is divided according to exceptionality, it is important to remember we are talking about children with a handicap, or giftedness, rather than a category of children per se. The type of exceptionality is of minimal importance. The key point is for students to understand the self-monitoring process, as well as to have sufficient motivation to implement it.

We will consider major classifications only in a general sense, recognizing that each area includes diverse children who share differing degrees of a similar condition. There is simply no substitute for individualization and common sense in applying self-monitoring.

Suggestions made here may be relevant to more than one exceptionality, but are usually mentioned in the area in which they have the most applicability. Also, many ideas are applicable across the entire spectrum of exceptional conditions. For example, all school-aged handicapped students have an individualized education program (IEP). Many gifted do as well, depending on state law. This is important because the IEP provides a formal vehicle for structuring a self-monitoring program. The student can even sign his or her name to the document, agreeing to the process. Parents also have an opportunity to sign the IEPs, thus acknowledging their support. Cooperative parents can contribute significantly to self-monitoring by rewarding successful participation at home. Parents may also decide to use self-monitoring to improve their own behavior.

Mentally Retarded

Mental retardation refers to "significantly sub-average general intellectual functioning existing concurrently with deficits in adaptive behavior, and manifested during the developmental period" (Grossman, 1973, p. 11). In essence, it implies a serious deficit in the cognitive, or mental, processes. There are also numerous levels of severity, ranging from mild to profound. Without engaging in a complex discussion of learning characteristics, it is sufficient to recognize that many retarded persons, especially those in the mild and moderate range, can benefit from self-monitoring.

Jackson and Boag (1981) review the pertinent literature with respect to using self-monitoring with the mentally retarded. They reported that most efficacy studies do not reveal a high degree of success, although considerable skill has been demonstrated by students in several studies. There could be several explanations for the mixed results. First, it is conceivable that considerable differences existed among the functioning levels of retarded students who participated. This is supported by the work of Nathan, Millham, Chilcutt, and Atkinson (1980), in which mildly retarded individuals were far more accurate self-monitors than moderately retarded ones. Second, subjects in some studies may not have been adequately prepared for self-monitoring. That is, they may not have understood the precise nature of their role as observer or of the behavior they were to observe. Further, students in the more successful studies might have had some degree of prior training or experience with self-monitoring.

There are several suggestions to facilitate the use of self-monitoring procedures by mentally retarded students. These include simplistic procedures for training and programming. Among the more common procedures are frequent repetition; short lessons, baseline periods, and intervention strategies; immediate rewards; consistency; concrete examples and rewards; and focusing on one behavior at a time. Basic practices emanating from a single concept are recommended. This recommendation is applicable to all children in terms of learning and implementing self-monitoring, but especially to those with retardation.

Self-monitoring can be used to teach functional skills to retarded students in practically every area of the curriculum. General topics include prevocational and vocational training, academics, activities of daily living, affective growth, and physical development. Specific topics include proper use of food utensils, teeth brushing, toileting, reduction of self-stimulating behaviors, and alternative communication systems (e.g., manual signing). The choice of topic is not as critical in the use of self-monitoring as is breaking down each skill into its most simplistic components. For this reason, task analysis is an important competency for teachers who use self-monitoring with their retarded students.

Self-monitoring can be used to teach each distinct behavior in a task analytic sequence. In this way, a retarded child can conceivably be taught a relatively complex behavior. The time required when self-monitoring is used for this purpose may be surprisingly small in some instances. That is, the baseline period may last only a few hours or one day rather than the normally expected one- to three-week period. The difference is in the simplicity of the task (e.g., sitting on a chair versus reduction of nail biting).

When using task analysis to teach retarded students, several suggestions are pertinent (Heward & Orlansky, 1980). These include: (1) limiting the task to a simple behavior; (2) defining the task in observable terms; (3) using a form of communication the child can understand; (4) being sure the task is something the child can and will do when prompted; and (5) focusing on the task instead of the child.

The last item in Heward and Orlansky's model, focusing on the behavior rather than the child, is important because it allows the teacher to be success oriented. This is recommended because most retarded children have experienced a considerable amount of failure in their lives. Rather than burden them with the possibility of more failure, focus is placed on the task instead. This same logic applies to other handicapped conditions as well.

The positive versus negative argument has implications for selection of target behaviors as well. It is usually preferable to increase a desirable behavior (e.g., brushing teeth three times a day) instead of decreasing a negative one (e.g., wetting pants less

Special Implications for Exceptional Students

often). Most behaviors can be defined in positive terms. This sometimes requires some creative thinking by the teacher.

A few other ideas are appropriate when using self-monitoring with retarded students. These include the following:

1. It is often advisable to use tokens as possible rewards for successful counting or as contingencies for improvement. Many children will probably have used tokens previously and thus understand their implied value.

2. A simple contingency contract might be useful, especially for some of the mildly retarded students. Including cooperative parents in the contract is often advisable.

3. The ability of retarded children to participate in the self-monitoring should be acknowledged. "Nothing ventured, nothing gained" is an appropriate axiom.

4. Simple counting procedures for the moderately retarded include placing rings on pegs, putting pieces in puzzles, putting pegs in pegboards, transferring jelly beans between pockets, and adding beads to a string. The idea is to keep the system as simple as possible. Also, it is sometimes helpful to use a counting system with which the child is familiar. Taking advantage of previous learning not only facilitates the task but also utilizes a familiar, positive behavior.

Learning Disabled

Self-monitoring probably has more potential for working with learning-disabled students than for any other exceptionality, with the possible exception of the gifted. A learning disability refers to a

> disorder in one or more of the basic psychological processes involved in understanding or in using language, spoken or written, which may manifest itself in an imperfect ability to listen, think, speak, read, write, spell, or do mathematical calculations. The term includes such conditions as perceptual handicaps, brain injury, minimal brain dysfunction, dyslexia, and developmental aphasia. The term does not include children who have learning problems which are primarily the result of visual, motor, or hearing handicaps, of mental retardation, or of environmental, cultural, or economic disadvantages. [P.L. 94-142, Section 5 (b) (4)]

In short, the term refers to children who have a severe discrepancy between ability and achievement in one or more academic skills or curriculum areas. By most definitions, these children also have average or above-average intellectual skills. Therefore, they should be able to successfully participate in self-monitoring. The only caution is that an adjustment may need to be made to accommodate the specific learning disability: A learning-disabled child who is being taught to use self-monitoring should be trained via a learning mode other than the deficit area. That is, if a child has difficulty learning by reading, the concept should be explained verbally. With other children, it may be possible to develop a reading lesson that teaches the child how to use self-monitoring. The reverse may also be true; that is, self-monitoring can be used to teach a learning disabled child to read. In this case, reading (or a component of reading, such as reading comprehension) can be taught using self-monitoring.

Self-monitoring is one of the few teaching approaches that allows a learning-disabled child to work on his or her own without fear of failure in front of someone in an authority or peer position. This is important because most of these children have learned to avoid situations in which their handicap is highly visible.

Many learning-disabled children experience social and emotional problems as a result of their handicap. Other frequent problems include hyperactivity, distractibility, and communication disorders. Deficits in these areas can often be successfully corrected or improved with self-monitoring.

Because of their intellectual skills, learning-disabled students are often excellent tutors in teaching self-monitoring to peers. This is particularly true when they have learned to use the system and when they desire to assist others.

Parents of learning-disabled youth are often keenly interested in their children's progress. Including them in a self-monitoring program may prove to be particularly useful.

Visually Impaired

Children who are visually impaired include both the blind and the partially sighted. These children are unable to learn through the visual modality. These individuals need to be taught through other sensory avenues, particularly auditory and tactile. Special aids such as braille, the Optacon®, and a tape recorder can enhance communication skills. Conversely, visually impaired students can also learn to use these aids through self-monitoring. Other curriculum areas that can be taught via self-monitoring include practical living skills, vocational competencies, physical development, and mobility training. In essence, visually impaired children can use self-monitoring to improve practically any behavior that sighted children can.

Hearing Impaired

We will define *hearing impaired* in the same manner as visual impairment. That is, these children are unable to use the hearing modality as a primary method for learning. Therefore, they have to rely heavily on the visual and tactile senses.

The most difficult problem encountered by most hearing-impaired children is acquisition of verbal language. As a result, they often have to learn auxiliary or alternative methods of communication. Two common methods include sign language and speech reading. The latter is sometimes referred to as lipreading or oral communication.

In addition to traditional curriculum areas, hearing impaired children can use self-monitoring to learn manual signs, improve oral communication, use a new hearing aid, and acquire a wide range of other skills. For example, self-monitoring can be useful for motivating these children; improving vocational competencies, work habits, and manipulative skills; and fostering affective and physical development.

A recent development in the field of hearing impairment is increased use of hearing ear dogs. These animals could be useful in alerting deaf children when an electronic counter reminds them of the need to record a target behavior. Self-monitoring could also be used to train hearing-impaired children to handle a hearing ear dog properly.

Communication Disordered

This area of exceptionality primarily involves students with impairments in speech or language. Van Riper (1972) defined a speech disorder as one that draws unfavorable attention to itself, interferes with communication, or causes the speaker to be socially maladjusted. It is also affected by a person's age. That is, an eighteen-year-old speaks quite differently than a three-year-old, but the speech of each might be considered appropriate for the respective developmental level.

Language disorders occur when a child is seriously deficient in the use of written or spoken systems that are normally intended for communication. Speech is one component of language—the spoken part.

Teachers who have in their classes children who exhibit speech and language problems should refer them to a speech therapist. Personally attempting a remediation effort could conceivably result in irreparable harm to the child. For example, calling attention to some communication problems, such as stuttering, tends to increase anxiety and thus intensifies the problem.

A speech therapist might be able to use self-monitoring as a practical tool for working with communication-disordered children. In fact, of all therapeutic approaches, self-monitoring offers one particularly unique advantage: Children can work independently on a targeted speech or language disorder without calling undue attention to it. In essence, the anxiety that intensifies most disorders in this area can be minimized because the conditions under which therapy is practiced are largely controlled by the individual. Furthermore, the individual can have significant input into designing the system (e.g., selecting the target behavior, identifying possible rewards, and establishing the baseline period).

Physically Handicapped

Physically handicapped students include those with orthopedic or other health impairments that are sufficiently severe to require special modifications in the school environment in order for them to receive an appropriate education. The term includes a wide range of physical aberrations, including such well-known problems as cerebral palsy, arthritis, epilepsy, cancer, muscular dystrophy, multiple sclerosis, cystic fibrosis, spina bifida, hydrocephaly, and osteomyelitis.

Self-monitoring can be used by practically all these children, provided that severe retardation is not present and that the child has the physical ability to activate a counting device. Considering the technological and prosthetic aids currently available to physically handicapped students, it is difficult to imagine a limitation so severe that an operable counting apparatus could not be designed. Simple devices can be activated by eye blinks, foot movements, tongue protrusions, tube blowing, or even biofeedback. Therefore, self-monitoring is a realistic approach for practically all physically handicapped students. The only possible limitations might be a teacher's inability to design a creative self-monitoring system based on a particular student's physical abilities.

When selecting an appropriate counting and recording instrument, the teacher should consider a child's current level of manipulative skills. For example, the extent to which a child can move his or her fingers to properly grip a pencil or pointer or to mash a pushbutton is important. It is also essential to identify body parts that afford the greatest degree of motor control.

Provided that cognitive skills are reasonably functional, a physically handicapped child should find self-monitoring to be useful. For example, the process can be used to improve mobility. It can also be used to teach children to operate prosthetic devices, wheelchairs, and crutches, as well as a wide range of other skills.

One of the more interesting uses of self-monitoring in the physical domain is to cope with such problems as tics (i.e., nervous twitches in a muscle) or even epilepsy. In fact, many psychosomatic illnesses can be improved through self-monitoring. For example, if a person's ulcers are aggravated or caused by stress, self-monitoring can be directed at helping the person cope with the problems producing the condition.

Behavior Disordered

Behavior-disordered students are those individuals whose environmental demands exceed their ability to cope successfully. These persons are sometimes referred to as *emotionally conflicted* or *emotionally disturbed*. The handicapping condition includes a wide range of abnormal behaviors, ranging in intensity from mild to severe. A vast majority of these individuals are in touch with reality and can relate to items and people in their environment. Others, however, particularly those with psychotic conditions, may actually pose a physical danger to themselves, to others, or to property. Those in the latter group may be largely unable to monitor their own behavior effectively.

Self-monitoring is primarily designed for those individuals in the mild to moderate range of behavior disorders who are able to relate to a select number of significant others. In fact, self-monitoring may be preferred for many of these students because it allows them to structure and control their own intervention program. In some cases, this control may represent the first time students have had personal responsibility over any aspect of their lives. The fact that they can control even one aspect of their behavior, however briefly, may lead to efforts to gain control in a positive way over other components of their lives.

Although the efficacy of self-monitoring for behavior-disordered students may depend to some degree on the level of severity, there is evidence that the process has been useful with certain subpopulations of these individuals (McLaughlin, 1977; Polsgrove, 1979). It may be that self-monitoring can often be achieved with little or no interaction by others. This phenomenon could be important to behavior-disordered children who have exhibited antisocial tendencies.

Parents of behavior-disordered students can also support the self-monitoring process in the home. A frequent complaint of behavior specialists is that it is difficult to apply their intervention program in the home. Self-monitoring may assist in this respect if: (1) parents and teachers communicate regularly about the process; (2) the child understands his or her behavior is being routinely checked by parents; and (3) sufficient motivation exists to encourage compliance.

Many inappropriate behaviors exhibited by behavior-disordered students are highly charged with emotion. When certain behaviors occur, the student and others in the environment may experience an emotional reaction. For example, one aggressive child had a tendency to hit his classmates forcefully from behind with his fist. A fight usually resulted. Other examples are less extreme (e.g., calling a friend by an uncomplimentary name, referring to a friend's mother in an unflattering sense, being insubordinate to the teacher). With emotional behaviors of this nature, a natural tendency is to address or analyze the situation in an affective sense. A teacher may ask such questions as What caused the child to behave in this manner? What can I do to respond? How can I deal with my reciprocal anger? While these reactions are normal, self-monitoring allows the teacher to focus (through the child) on the behavior *per se*, and not on the more complex and often confusing affective considerations.

Self-monitoring can be used to address a wide variety of inappropriate behaviors. Examples include public masturbation, social isolation, temper tantrums, aggression, hyperactivity, distractibility, property destruction, and stealing. The list is virtually endless, limited only by the experiences of a particular teacher. Inappropriate behaviors can be reduced using a direct self-monitoring system or a more indirect approach. For example, the skill of modeling desirable behaviors can be taught in a general sense. Once students become proficient at modeling proper behaviors (e.g., in a role-playing situation), these can then be substituted for inappropriate ones.

The basic tenets of self-monitoring, with the exception of counting and recording one's own behavior, can even be applied with severely behavior-disordered children. The exception is noted because an adjustment may be needed with these children. Counting and recording can be done by a second party (e.g., peer, teacher, parent). With this approach, behaviors such as self-mutilation and echolalia can often be improved.

Reliability checks are often important with mildly and moderately behavior-disordered students. This is not necessarily due to a need for accuracy but because it forms the framework for counseling. With agreements (or disagreements) serving as a common ground for communication, a teacher (or counselor) and student can constructively discuss specific behaviors, possible causes, and eventual consequences.

Gifted and Talented

According to the *Congressional Record* (1978), gifted and talented children are those who:

> are identified at the preschool, elementary, or secondary level as possessing demonstrated or potential abilities that give evidence of high performance capability in areas such as intellectual, creative, specific academic or leaderability, or in the performing and visual arts, and who by reason thereof require services or activities not ordinarily provided by the school. (H-12179)

Self-monitoring offers opportunities for gifted and talented students to explore and develop specialized interests, skills, and abilities. Once they learn the system, they can often proceed to design and implement highly individualized approaches. They are limited only by their creativity and identification of realistic rewards. The process toward a goal is often sufficient reward in itself.

One particularly challenging activity is to convert undesirable behaviors to positive ones. We mentioned earlier that this can usually be done but often requires creative thinking. During the training phase, a teacher may wish to list several negative behaviors and ask students to redefine them in positive terms.

Many gifted and talented students enjoy working alone without a lot of supervision. Once they have mastered basic self-monitoring skills, the process certainly affords them this opportunity. For example, a student may desire to devote more time to his coin collection and less time to television. Regardless of the objective, self-monitoring is usually a helpful device for promoting desirable behavior.

While many of their assets are highly visible, gifted and talented students may attempt to hide deficit areas. Yet, practically everyone, regardless of skill level, has some areas of relative weakness. Self-monitoring allows these students to work on strengthening deficiencies without calling undue attention to them. That is, a self-monitoring program can be designed that does not require peer awareness or support.

Gifted and talented students might particularly enjoy the use of microcomputers to count and record target behaviors. Not only does this approach provide a highly accurate and easily interpreted format for pertinent data (e.g., coded bar graph), but also encourages students to improve their skills in computer usage.

Self-monitoring might have special utility for teaching gifted and talented students to improve their creative talents. While some argument might exist over whether creativity can be taught, there is certainly support for at least allowing children to develop their natural skills in this area. When the goal is to improve a creative behavior through self-monitoring, it is usually advisable to employ a behavior rating scale instead of a common checklist to record data. For example, if an artistically talented child wants to improve her ability to paint color portraits, the fact that she paints a certain number of portraits may not be crucial. What is important is the quality of each one. Hence, a rating scale would yield far more valuable comparative information. For additional information on the use of self-monitoring with creative behaviors, the reader is referred to the chapter in this book on covert and personal behaviors. Similar rules apply to both areas.

Parents of gifted and talented students may be particularly valuable in implementing a self-monitoring program. Not only are they usually interested in their children's progress, but they are often in a position of assisting with rewards. For example, many desirable rewards fall under the parents' jurisdiction (e.g., personal home computer, dating freedom, use of the family car). Students could also teach their parents to use self-monitoring.

One word of caution is in order with respect to gifted students being taught to use self-monitoring. Teachers and parents have a natural tendency to assume that many of these children learn more rapidly and easily than they actually do. Therefore, there is a possibility during the training period that a teacher may falsely believe that a student has mastered a particular step when in actuality he or she has not. Or, the teacher could skip a step in the process and assume the student understood what was done. Because the student feels that he or she is considered so bright, he or she does not want to ask questions and look "stupid" in front of peers. The point is to cover each step thoroughly, repeat frequently, and review until complete mastery is achieved. The teacher should not make assumptions, regardless of how intelligent a child appears to be.

Conclusion

Self-monitoring is useful for children who function at all levels of the developmental spectrum, with the possible exception of a few who have severe mental or emotional disorders. In most instances, handicapping conditions merely result in the need to use special adaptations for counting and recording behavior.

In the first four chapters of this book we have attempted to provide an overview of the self-monitoring process. Our discussions have focused on basic components of self-monitoring, as well as the populations with whom it has applicability. We will now proceed to introduce a more practical perspective—how self-monitoring can be used in the daily lives of children and youth.

Section II
Specific Applications

INTRODUCTION

While Section One focused on general aspects of self-monitoring, Section Two is concerned with applying principles of the process to specific problem behaviors. A major resource for practical ideas presented in this section is the research literature.

The research literature in self-monitoring has been basically nontechnical in nature, primarily directed toward solving practical problems found in most classrooms. These problems include deficient academic behaviors, such as keeping distractible students on-task, teaching impulsive students to complete tasks, training students to improve study habits, helping students with written and verbal expression, and utilizing self-grading to reduce time demands on teachers and to give more immediate feedback following student assignments.

Other chapters are concerned with teaching disruptive students to monitor and control their behavior, training students to increase work productivity, and teaching children self-care skills such as proper showering and clothing care. Ideas are also presented for students who desire to improve some aspect of their personal and/or private lives with self-monitoring (e.g., weight gain or loss, interpersonal relations, anxiety, depression).

The final chapter is designed to provide the "finishing touches" for teachers, parents, counselors, and other individuals who are concerned with teaching the self-monitoring process. The ultimate goal is for students to successfully initiate, implement, and evaluate their own self-monitoring programs. In this way students can break the bond of dependence upon the self-monitoring process and become "masters of their fate."

The efficiency of one's present approaches to self-management can be readily examined by reviewing the success of last New Year's resolutions. These attempts at self-management are sometimes made jokingly and at other times made in earnest. It is bordering on rudeness to ask how someone intends to accomplish such goals as losing twenty pounds, becoming physically fit, spending more time with family or loved ones, or studying or writing more frequently. The reason is that the individual probably does not have any more than vague ideas as to methods he or she will use. The public announcement may, in itself, be the only method known (establishing social reinforcers for behaviors approaching the goal and/or punishers for unproductive behavior). The person who masters the art of self-monitoring is much better prepared to change behavior systematically and to achieve personal goals.

Chapter 5
ACADEMIC BEHAVIORS

Self-monitoring can be used with academic skills for three major purposes. The first is to reduce teacher time required for data collection while using proven, reinforcement-based, behavior change programs directed by the teacher. The second is to increase general (e.g., staying on task) and specific (e.g., number of math problems worked completely, sentences written, phonics worksheets completed) academic behaviors through self-monitoring's reactive effect. These possible changes are usually attributable to conditioned reinforcers or punishers associated with the process of recording one's own behavior. Satisfaction derived from reviewing one's behavioral chart is a good example. Positive changes can also be derived from unplanned social reinforcers, such as when a friend says how proud he or she is of progress being made. A third goal of self-monitoring is to teach to students management skills that are not dependent on the teacher. These skills can be generalized beyond a specific classroom to a variety of settings. For example, a child who masters the multiplication tables through self-monitoring may decide to use the same process to decrease time spent watching television.

The most common behaviors investigated by self-monitoring researchers have been classroom functions referred to as *on-task responses*. This refers to the ability of a student to focus attention on a specific task, such as putting a puzzle together or reading a story. A second general academic behavior that has often been researched is assignment completion. Specific academic skills for which self-monitoring has been used most frequently include penmanship, creative writing, mathematics, and reading.

Self-monitoring has been used successfully with data collection, as well as general and specific academic behaviors. Perhaps it would be useful to examine closely several key studies from the professional literature. A selected sampling is summarized below. Along with each topic is a vignette, the purpose of which is to illustrate the practicality of using self-monitoring. A short section on instructional implications is also included after each study.

General Academic Skills

These skills include staying on-task, completing assignments, and studying. Proficiency in these skills does not necessarily guarantee success in academic areas. However, these skills certainly appear to be supportive of success.

Task-Related Behaviors

Workman, Helton, and Watson (1982) reported that self-monitoring programs may reflect maintenance of teacher-administered consequences that have been previously successful. Their study used self-monitoring with a four-year-old who had no previous exposure to a structured behavior management program. It also addressed whether changes in the ecosystem of the classroom (e.g., teacher attention) may be the cause of reactivity often associated with self-monitoring applied to four different often associated with self-monitoring. The study used ten-second intervals with self-monitoring applied to four different categories of behavior. These categories included: (1) sustained schoolwork; (2) compliance with teacher requests (e.g., completed at least one assignment per time interval); (3) adult social attention of a nonaversive nature (e.g., physical or verbal attention to subject which was judged neutral or positive); and (4) adult social attention of an aversive nature (e.g., physical or verbal attention to subject that was judged to be negative).

The procedure for self-monitoring was that a timer was set at five-minute intervals. The student marked a piece of paper indicating whether she was working on teacher-assigned tasks. Self-monitoring was only directed to sustained school work, using a piece of paper taped on the wall near the student's desk. Results showed an increase in sustained school work, as well as compliance with teacher requests. Increases in compliance were noted during the self-monitoring phase, indicating that sustained school work and compliance are a part of a class responses. That is, one behavior tends to be affected by changes in the other.

Although positive adult attention was related to changes in sustained school work and compliance, teacher attention was not totally responsible for these changes. The relationship was not direct. Positive attention after baseline never dropped.

INSTRUCTIONAL IMPLICATIONS The Workman et al. study indicated that self-monitoring without planned consequences can dramatically improve on-task behavior and compliance with teacher requests. It also showed that time-sampling techniques can be used with students as young as four years of age. Additionally, there was evidence that improvements in on-task and compliance behavior resulted in increases in positive teacher attention. This probably accounted in some measure for the changes attributed to reactivity. Merely recording behavior every five minutes on a wall chart, whether one is on task or not, may be followed by increased compliance with teacher requests. The increase in positive teacher attention has broad applicability for students who have trouble staying on task.

Sagotsky, Patterson, and Lepper (1978) used self-monitoring with sixty-seven fifth- and sixth-grade students. They used five locational measures of on-task behavior, which included: (1) at seat working; (2) at teachers' desk; (3) at seat not working; (4) out of seat not working; and (5) out of room. They also used one academic measure: the number of problems correctly completed.

The self-monitoring procedure involved each student being given a sheet of paper with space to mark where his or her workbook progress stopped each day. Each student also received a paper with twelve empty boxes. They were told to note from time to time whether or not they actually were working on math units. They were to put a + in a box if they were and a - in the box if they were not. They were also told a - should serve as a reminder to resume studying. Results indicated self-monitoring increased on-task behavior significantly. Self-monitoring also increased the average number of problems done correctly.

INSTRUCTIONAL IMPLICATIONS The Sagotsky et al. investigation utilized an extremely simple time-sampling technique without a timing device or audio cue to interrupt classwork. Students can use simple self-monitoring with a notecard or a sheet of paper resembling that in Figure 5-1 taped on or near their desk.

Barkley, Copeland, and Sivage (1980) used self-monitoring

[ ][ ][ ][ ]

[ ][ ][ ][ ]

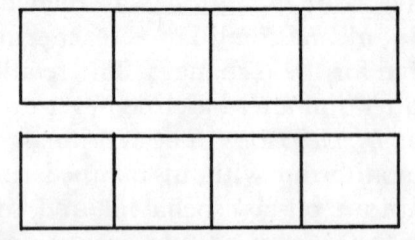

Instructions: When you think of it, put a plus (+) in each box if you are working or a minus (-) if you are not. This is to be done only during class time.

Figure 5-1. A recording sheet for monitoring on- and off-task behavior.

with six subjects, seven to ten years old, who were considered hyperactive and impulsive. The researchers used recording cards, a poster with five rules for staying on task, and a tape recorder with bell set at randomly programmed intervals. Each student marked a check if he or she was on task when the bell rang. Bells were rung at average intervals of three minutes. Students received points for being on task. They also earned bonus points for accuracy, which was checked by being in agreement with independent observers.

Results indicated that five of six students increased on-task performance. This success could be related to self-monitoring, or it could be attributed to the prearranged contingency for on-task behavior that also existed during intervention.

INSTRUCTIONAL IMPLICATIONS. The Barkley et al. study demonstrated that self-monitoring can be used along with an existing reinforcement system for on-task behavior. Self-monitoring may assist some students in earning reinforcers for staying on task. Also, self-monitoring may save teacher time by shifting the responsibility for data collection to the student. However, bonus points for accuracy and/or penalties for inaccuracy are a necessary component when earned reinforcers are based on self-motivated data.

Broden, Hall, and Mitts (1971) used self-monitoring with an eighth-grade female student to improve her on-task behavior. She was observed prior to and during self-monitoring for ten-second intervals over a thirty-minute period in a history class. The investigators used the term *study* when referring to the desired behaviors. Study behaviors included facing the teacher, writing lecture notes, facing a student answering a teacher question, and reciting when called upon by the teacher. These behaviors are often referred to as *on-task responses*. The same observation applies to the investigators' use of the term nonstudy behaviors (e.g., being out of seat, talking without teacher recognition, facing the window, fingering makeup or comb, working on assignments from another class). These are typically labeled *off-task behaviors*.

The subject began self-monitoring using a slip of paper with three rows of ten squares each, a place for the date, and instructions to record on-task behavior "when she thought of it." Each time she was on-task she put a + in the square. Conversely, she put a – when she was not. This form of self-monitoring led to a dramatic increase in on-task behavior. Baseline conditions were reintroduced, and the behavior again returned to low levels. When self-monitoring was reinstated, the on-task percentage dramatically increased again, except for two days when recording slips were not issued. Later, self-monitoring was paired with teacher praise, leading to a slight increase in desired behaviors. On-task behaviors eventually stabilized around 90 percent of the time. Praise without self-monitoring was also attempted, leading to a decrease below 80 percent. When both self-monitoring and praise were withdrawn, after the research was completed, on-task behavior stabilized around 80 percent. This compared to 30 percent during the baseline period.

INSTRUCTIONAL IMPLICATIONS. The program used by Broden et al. is another example of a student merely marking on a slip of paper with thirty squares on it a + or – for on- or off-task behavior "when she thought of it." This study may have been a model for the Sagotsky et al. investigation.

The recording technique gives the reader specific criteria for on-task behaviors (e.g., facing the teacher, writing lecture notes, facing a student answering a teacher question, reciting when called upon by the teacher) and off-task behaviors (e.g., being out of seat, talking without teacher recognition, facing the windows, fingering makeup or comb, working on assignments from another class). Although these criteria are designed for an individual student in a specific class, they could be adapted to other students and classroom settings. Specific criteria such as these could prove useful in self-monitoring on-task behavior.

In conclusion, on-task behavior can best be self-monitored using some form of time sampling. Students may record their behavior each time a bell or timer rings, or randomly when they think of it. It would appear that when the purpose of self-monitoring is merely to increase on-task behavior, without receiving reinforcers based on the self-monitored data, the random method should be used. When self-monitored data is used to earn reinforcers, the bell or timer should be used to allow reliability checks by the teacher.

> Susan was a young six-year-old, halfway through her first year of school. She was certainly bright enough to do the work but often became distracted by irrelevant stimuli. Susan's teacher decided to try self-monitoring with her. An eight-and one-half-inch by eleven-inch wall chart was placed on the wall next to Susan's desk. An electronic kitchen timer was set to ring at undesignated intervals. Whenever Susan was doing her work when it rang, she was allowed to give herself a gold star. Distractions were noted by an **X**. Each **X** was also used as a signal to return to work. The goal was to earn a gold star in 80 percent of the cases over a one-month period. No reward was used other than verbal reinforcement. Immediate improvement was noted as the baseline began. Whenever improvement began to wane (as measured by two consecutive **X**s), the teacher reminded her of the necessity to stay on task. Also, a day of all gold stars was ended with a hug. The plan was explained to the rest of the class the day it began. Several other students wanted a chance to earn gold stars. The teacher allowed voluntary participation by the others, provided they selected a desirable target behavior.

Assignment Completion

Piersall and Kratchowill (1979) investigated assignment completion with two different students. Their first student was Susan, seven years of age, who failed to complete phonics assignments.

The researchers recorded the percentage of correct items on daily phonics worksheets. They employed self-monitoring by using a card taped inside the student's desk on which she kept records of scores provided by her teacher. Results indicated an increase from 30 percent to 65 percent correct during the self-monitoring.

Their second case involved Ken, fifteen years of age, who failed to complete assignments in reading and math. The investigators recorded, in reading, the number of SRA units completed and, in math, the number of assignments completed. An accuracy level of 75 percent was required for a piece of work to qualify as a completed assignment. Ken also recorded the number of SRA or math assignments completed on a piece of notebook paper. During baseline he averaged zero assignments completed in both subjects. During self-monitoring he completed one or more assignments almost every day (e.g., 16/32 SRA; 10/12 math).

INSTRUCTIONAL IMPLICATIONS. Students can use notecards to monitor assignments completed with accuracy criteria as shown in Figures 5-2 and 5-3. The success of these self-monitoring techniques as measured by assignment completion may be due to the students' receiving social praise from teachers for small improvements. It could also be due to the visual evidence of improvement now available to students. Factors such as receiving adult praise and seeing visual evidence of improvement should be incorporated into self-monitoring programs to increase assignment completion.

> Wayne was an active sixteen-year-old who had a problem completing homework assignments. His intentions were good, but it always appeared that more enjoyable activities were available (e.g., television, dating, visiting friends). He wanted to go to college after graduation, but his grades were then too low. He decided to ask a friend in the honor society for a suggestion. His friend suggested that Wayne design a recording chart, with a daily space for each area in which he usually received homework. Then they agreed that homework had to be done from four to six o'clock in the afternoon, Sunday through Thursday. This left him evenings and weekends to spend time on other activities.

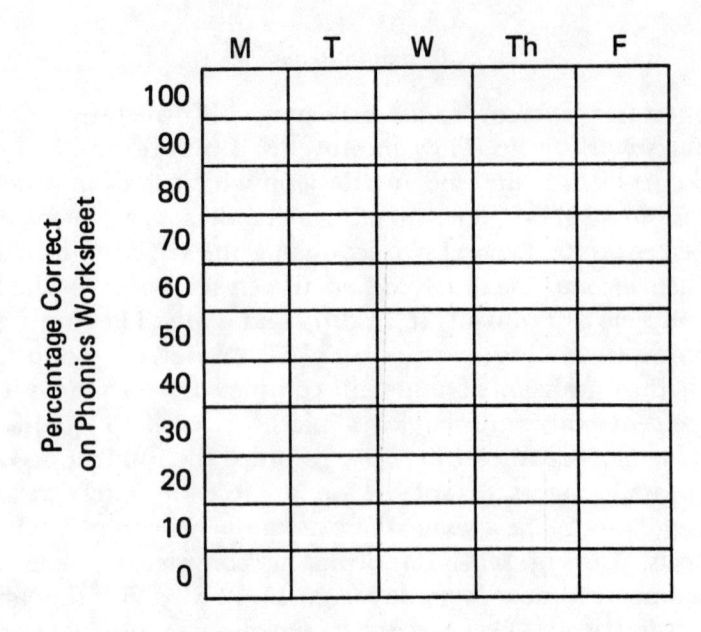

Instructions: Put an X at the percent marked by the teacher each day on your phonics worksheet.

Figure 5-2. Self-monitoring card for recording percentage completed and correct assignments.

Instructions: Write the number of assignments completed with at least 75 percent correct for each school day.

Figure 5-3. Self-monitoring card for recording number of assignments completed with at least 75 percent accuracy.

Wayne's parents cooperated with him on his project. They agreed to install a new muffler system in his car if he could attain a 95 percent completion record for a six-week period. Furthermore, failure to attain an 80 percent completion record would result in forfeiture of his driving privileges for a month. Spot checks between parents and teachers were allowed to monitor for accuracy. Results were excellent, with a 97 percent completion record over the six-week period. Social reinforcement from parents was also useful in serving to maintain progress.

Study Behavior

Hefferman and Richards (1981) examined self-control of study behavior. They used two groups of undergraduate students in their study. One group had serious study problems (i.e., less than ten hours of studying per week for a semester). These students were interested in making a concerted effort to improve their study skills. The second group of students were classified as having already developed successful strategies.

Successful students were interviewed and observed to determine how their procedures worked. Then these naturally occurring techniques were applied to the other group of forty-five students with study problems. Naturally occurring successful study techniques included arranging for rewards following studying (used by 75 percent of the students), self-monitoring of some form (83 percent of the students), and stimulus control (100 percent typically isolated themselves while studying).

When these techniques were applied with the group of forty-five students with poor study habits, an increased grade average was noted. An increased grade average was also noted when compared to a third group of students who received standard instruction in study skills (problem solving and good study habits).

INSTRUCTIONAL IMPLICATIONS. Although students in this study were undergraduates, similar strategies can be applied with younger students. Undergraduate students are often faced with a difficult test of their study behavior since they are frequently living away from home for the first time with many highly reinforcing alternatives available. When these students were living at home they may have had much of their study behavior controlled by their parents, as well as having less access to the type of reinforcers available away from home. Undergraduate students who develop successful study behaviors are often doing so under difficult circumstances.

Younger students can apply these same techniques. Proper study behaviors are increasingly important to younger students for two reasons. The first reason is that homework is being required of younger students each year. The second reason is the increasing number of families in which both parents work or only one is present. This often reduces a parent's ability to supervise study behavior.

Three common techniques to increase study behavior and ultimately improve grades are: (1) establishing time periods and locations that are isolated for study purposes (e.g., library, bedroom); (2) employing some form of self-monitoring (e.g., number of correct math homework problems, number of pages read, number of study questions answered correctly; and (3) linking the self-monitored behavior with a preferred activity or other reinforcer (e.g., tweny correct problems allows the student to watch a favorite television program).

Judy despised studying for most tests because they required memorization. History and biology were particularly annoying because of the lists she had to learn. She was unhappy with her attitude and decided to use self-monitoring. Her program was simple. For each concentrated study session of forty-five minutes, she awarded herself with either a hot bath or a bowl of ice cream. She also recorded each successful session with a yellow mark in her diary on the appropriate date. Ten yellow marks could be converted to the purchase of a desired clothing item not to exceed twenty-five dollars. She also reluctantly agreed to donate five dollars of allowance money to her favorite charity for each test score under 80 percent. On her first two tests after deciding to use self-monitoring, Judy made a 74 percent and a 78 percent. She was not sure if the system was worthwhile. Cheating on herself would have been easy. She could have even waited another week before beginning. Her willpower was dwindling until she told her boyfriend about her program to improve studying behavior. He was impressed and suggested they use the program together and reward each other for accuracy, improvements in study behavior, and better test scores. Their teacher was impressed with their progress and asked what they were doing differently. They smiled and replied they were studying together.

Specific Academic Skills

Specific academic skills addressed here include handwriting, written expression, arithmetic, and reading. Results and techniques can also be applied to other academic areas.

Handwriting

Jones, Trap, and Cooper (1977) used self-monitoring with twenty-two first graders in the area of penmanship. Students were taught handwriting for three months using paper, pencil, board, and chalk to achieve a 75 percent mastery level prior to the study. This was necessary to have the prior skills required to use evaluative overlays employed in the study. Students were taught to use overlays in two to five days in work sessions of fifteen to twenty minutes. Evaluative overlays were initially described by Helwig, Jones, Norman, and Cooper (1976).

The first skill required when using overlays is proper paper placement. Students learned to self-record their success in maneuvering samples with an overlay within a tolerance of one to three millimeters. Initial training ceased when students reached 75 percent agreement with the experimenter. Then students began self-monitoring with the overlay and no experimenter feedback. Students achieved 81 to 98 percent accuracy without feedback. Each student was matched with the overlay that yielded 50 percent correct handwriting prior to self-monitoring (i.e., one, two, or three millimeters tolerance).

Previous results using the Helwig et al. overlays indicated they required too much time for classroom teachers to be able to use them efficiently. The average rate of evaluation in this study had been four letters per minute after initial training. This time factor reduced normal advantages expected from the overlays (e.g., objectivity in scoring). A potential solution was found when the first graders learned to use overlays via self-monitoring within 80-120 minutes of instruction and practice. Students then could do an overlay evaluation with considerably less teacher time and achieve high reliability averages when compared with trained observers (i.e., 79 percent in Group 1, 82 percent in Group 2, 84 percent in Group 3). This objective and immediate feedback using overlays can facilitate handwriting instruction. Similar handwriting results could be expected in self-monitoring of letter formation, connections, endings, and spacings using models of correct handwriting and scoring criteria in the place of evaluative overlays (Hansen, 1974).

INSTRUCTIONAL IMPLICATIONS. Handwriting is a particularly difficult skill to evaluate objectively. This can be evidenced by asking any two third-grade teachers to evaluate a particular student's cursive writing. Thus, the value of the described overlays is apparent. The teacher may make his or her own overlays from tagboard or use some other method of evaluation.

Haring, Eaton, Lovitt, and Hansen (1974) suggested a point or factor system. With manuscript letters, the formation, slant, and spacing are each worth one point for each letter. In evaluating cursive letters, the connectives or endings are added to the three measures for manuscript. Therefore, a three-letter word would have nine possible points for manuscript writing and twelve for cursive.

If the overlay or factor approach is used to evaluate handwriting, the process takes a great deal of teacher time. There is a long time lag between the writing and feedback. With trained students evaluating the writing by using either technique, both increased teacher time and more immediate feedback to students can be provided. Students graded subjectively never know what to expect. However, those whose handwriting is evaluated in a more objective, self-monitored method can practice correcting their errors.

> Hector was an eight-year-old who had been relatively slow in attaining developmental landmarks (e.g., walking, talking, crawling). His fine motor skills were rather poorly developed when his third-grade teacher began to introduce cursive writing. The daily drills were very

frustrating to Hector, who soon began to question his own ability in other areas. Hector's teacher decided self-monitoring might be useful. Therefore, she talked with him about a possible approach. Together, they decided that Hector needed thirty extra minutes of handwriting practice per day. Furthermore, he needed to check his work for accuracy, using the Helwig et al. overlays. An 80 percent accuracy level was required at all times. An unsatisfactory level of proficiency resulted in a repeated assignment. Each day that Hector worked satisfactorily on his handwriting he was given a token to bring home to his parents. The token was an affirmation of success and could be exchanged for thirty minutes of video-game time on a home computer. The program worked well despite Hector's physical limitations. Hector's success was also strengthened by doing a variety of small motor exercises and by receiving assistance from a peer tutor.

Written Expression

Ballard and Glynn (1975) worked with thirty-seven subjects, eight to eleven years of age, in New Zealand in the area of written expression. Fourteen were chosen for experimental purposes (data collection), while the rest constituted a control group. Four target behaviors included the number of sentences written, different action words, different describing words, and number of intervals on task. For purposes of clarification to the students, a sentence was operationally defined as beginning with a capital letter and/or on a new line, and/or having a period, question mark, or exclamation point at the end, and/or containing at least one subject and predicate. Action words were those that "expressed an act, occurrence, or movement, but not a mode of being." *Number of different describing words* was a combination of adjectives and adverbs, with an adjective "serving as the modifier of a noun to denote the quality of the thing named, to indicate quantity or extend, or to specify a noun as distinct from something else." An adverb was defined as "a word that modified a verb, adjective, another adverb, preposition, phrase, clause or sentence, and expressed some relation or manner of quality, time, place, degree, number, cause, opposition, affirmation, or denial"

(p. 389). On-task behavior was defined as the percentage of ten-second intervals observed during twenty-five minutes of writing time in which a child was writing with a pencil or had a pencil in contact with the paper, using an eraser, using a dictionary, looking at wall charts, or seeking teacher help by raising a hand.

Three wall charts were used. The first was a "good writing chart." It included suggestions for writing sentences, along with a description of the sentences, and use of describing words, with examples of describing words. The second was a "writing time chart." It offered suggestions concerning appropriate behavior during instruction, as well as general suggestions for identifying topics. The last chart was an "ideas" summary that provided specific topics for use in writing (e.g., horses, a farm).

Self-monitoring was accomplished using a daily counting sheet clipped to each student's story. For each story, he or she recorded on this sheet the number of sentences, different describing words, and different action words. After completing the assignment, each child transferred the counts to a final tally sheet fastened to story folders. This allowed each student to keep a permanent record of his or her daily performance on the three measures.

Self-monitoring by itself had little effect over baseline on each of the three measures. Reinforcement was then introduced sequentially for
1. Number of sentences written: One point per sentence could be exchanged for one minute of preferred activity time (e.g., games, art activities)
2. Number of different action words used: One point was given only for new action words and discontinued for number of sentences.
3. Number of different describing words only: One point per each describing word was given. During this part, no points were awarded for either of the other two measures.

When points were contingent upon number of sentences written, both number of sentences and number of describing words increased. As points were awarded for action words, their numbers increased while the other two measures dropped somewhat. When a shift was made to points for describing words, the results increased dramatically. On-task behavior increased with each of the reinforcement conditions over both the baseline and self-monitoring phases.

The children's stories were also independently assessed in a subjective manner by two lecturers on the English faculty of a local college. The professors' ratings correlated with the students' at 0.69 (out of a possible perfect correlation of 1.0). Ratings were higher for all reinforcement conditions, with the highest score given during reinforcement for different action words.

INSTRUCTIONAL IMPLICATIONS. The Ballard and Glynn (1975) study investigated a very complex skill. Written expression is often viewed as a talent that may be developed but is primarily innate. This is probably due to the inability of many teachers to teach the skill effectively. Teachers of written expression often provide models of classic novels or short stories in the hope that these will be sufficient. Successful attempts at copying the models receive teacher praise. Individuals who become competent writers may well be fortunate accidents, in which the right set of circumstances happened to occur at the right time.

This study provides several excellent attempts to provide the right set of circumstances to elementary-aged students. The wall charts provide antecedent stimuli to form sentences, suggest adjectives and adverbs, describe proper writing habits, and give general and specific topics for writing themes. The second set of circumstances is the self-monitoring techniques for recording the number of sentences, describing words, and action words. The ideas are quite similar to techniques used by Hemingway and other accomplished writers. These individuals used words or pages for self-monitoring instead of sentences. The last major strategy is to provide activity reinforcers for increases in sentences, describing words, and action words. This is very similar to Hemingway's rewarding himself for an especially successful day.

Wallace and Pear (1977) reported what a behavior manager, such as a teacher, might do to increase literary output from a writer who has prerequisite skills but who is unable to actually produce a novel. The authors cited Skinner (1953; 1957), Goldiamond (1965), and Kazdin (1974b). Specific suggestions included providing a well-lighted private work area with all the necessary writing materials, defining meaningful units of behavior (e.g., words, pages), and arranging supplementary reinforcers for completion of a number of units within a given time frame.

Several successful novelists unknowingly adopted many of these methods, including well-known Irving Wallace. Others have included Anthony Trollope, Arnold Bennett, Ernest Hemingway, and perhaps Victor Hugo. Most of these authors used self-monitoring in the form of daily counting of words or pages written. Hugo is said to have confined himself to his writing area by having his valet take away all his clothing until the hour he expected to complete a day's writing. Trollope wrote about his self-monitoring behavior, which offended critics. Hemingway told a reporter that he would put in extra work or write more words on a particular day so he would not feel guilty fishing in the Gulf Stream the next day. It would seem that all writers, from an elementary student in a language arts class to an accomplished author in fiction or nonfiction, could learn from these ideas.

Robert was a promising high school senior who had considerable promise as a creative writer. His raw skills were fairly well developed, but he lacked the self-discipline needed to develop his talent properly. Robert decided to try self-monitoring as a means of increasing his efforts. His initial attempt was to write a short book of 100 poems about nature. He established a schedule of one poem per day to be written in the morning before going to school. Each day that he was successful, he would allow himself a trip by the local delicatessen for a snack of his choice. For unsuccessful days, he decided to do without lunch. His basic idea was to take advantage of his fondness for eating. The book of poems was completed in 107 days, with illness and an unexpected visit by relatives creating the only problems. Robert was so pleased with his effort that he decided to use the same system for a book on fiction. This time his goal was to write three typewritten pages per day. Again, his fondness for food served as a strong motivator. His writing soon became an established habit.

Arithmetic

Hundert and Bucher (1978) employed student self-monitoring to save teacher time in grading arithmetic. They used four males with an average age of ten years, four months in their study. They reported that students self-monitored accurately when points were awarded based on self-rated scores. Individual improvements were also noted when points were later exchanged for prizes.

The investigators conducted a second experiment, using seventeen boys with an average age of fifteen years, three months. Here they attempted to maintain low levels of exaggerated performance when improvements were rewarded based on self-monitoring. They began with no control for accuracy, and students tended to inflate their scores. Next, checking procedures were adopted, and self-ratings were checked publicly. Bonus points were awarded for accuracy, and penalties imposed for inaccuracy. This was called the "maximum checks" condition. The procedure reduced the discrepancy between independent observers and self-monitoring for fifteen of seventeen pupils. Then a "minimum checks" condition was used, in which the self-rating accuracy of one random student who worked well was checked each day. The minimum checks maintained high levels of agreement with teacher scoring. No significant changes in arithmetic performance were reported as a result of self-monitoring. However, the teachers noted considerable savings in time spent scoring papers.

INSTRUCTIONAL IMPLICATIONS. This study investigated what students may do if their self-monitored performance is the basis of reward, as compared to teacher monitoring. Students tended to exaggerate or inflate their scores to receive reinforcers. A checking system employing bonus points for accurate self-monitoring and penalties for inaccurate self-monitoring was implemented. The checking was gradually reduced from checking every student every day to checking one random student every day. Accuracy was maintained when the one random student was checked. This sophisticated method of gradually reducing teacher checks can be used with any form of student self-evaluation or self-recording in which students earn reinforcers based upon self-monitored data. It can reduce teacher time in grading papers, a major after-school task.

> Marguerite was an eight-year-old third grader who had difficulty with long division. Her teacher was using a self-monitoring program with the class in order to allow

students to progress at their own pace. Each student was expected to work five problems per day, checking his or her work against an answer sheet. Grades were then recorded on a master list. All five problems had to be worked correctly before a student could move to the next level of difficulty. For each problem missed a student had to add two additional ones from an auxiliary sheet. The program seemed to work well for most of the students and for the teacher in particular. Marguerite, however, had considerable difficulty. Her problem was that she had never grasped the initial concept well enough to proceed. Marguerite was referred to a remedial arithmetic class specifically to work on long division. Here she worked at a much slower pace, with the assistance of several concrete teaching aids and a peer tutor. She later returned to the self-monitoring program and worked rather well, although her goal was reestablished at three problems per day.

Reading

Ruppel (1979) investigated four groups of deficient readers. One group used self-monitoring alone, while two groups used self-monitoring of comprehension questions following certain reading passages. The reading comprehension groups used some sort of reinforcement (usually instructors' approval) for either improvement over prior scores or exercise completion. The fourth group was used as a control. Two hundred and four undergraduate college students enrolled in a reading study skills course participated in the study. All three treatment groups using self-monitoring improved over the control group in passages completed, with the self-monitoring/task-completion group showing the greatest improvement. Reading comprehension levels were retained. These results, supportive of the self-monitoring process, might also be applied to secondary students with problems in reading.

INSTRUCTIONAL IMPLICATIONS. Ruppel (1979) demonstrated the value of self-monitoring for teaching reading comprehension. While this particular study focused on college-level students, there is reason to believe the procedure could also be used with students of other ages. Furthermore, if self-monitoring is effective with reading comprehension, it might also be useful with other reading skills such as syllabication, consonant blends, and homonyms.

Randy was a fourth grader who had been working in the SRA reading kit for three weeks. Although his progress was satisfactory, he was becoming somewhat disenchanted with the various stories. His primary interests were insects and airplanes. His teacher decided to use his favorite topics as an incentive to work in the SRA kit. She also allowed him to monitor his successful completion of SRA units. When Randy completed a new story in the SRA kit, she would allow him to read one article about insects or airplanes. When SRA work was unsatisfactory, he was not permitted free time to read about his favorite topics. At the end of a one-month period, Randy checked his overall success rate. His mother, at a conference with the teacher, had agreed that a 90 percent success rate would earn a trip to a local museum. Less than 90 percent success resulted in a decrease by one-half of his allowance for the next month. Randy used his system to maximum advantage and made substantial progress throughout the year.

Miscellaneous Factors

Some factors relate to the use of self-monitoring with academic skills that overlap both general and specific functions. These factors include self-selected versus other-selected contingencies and self-instruction.

Self-Selected Versus Other-Selected Contingencies

Who selects the reward, and what difference does it make in a person's overall performance? Several studies have indicated that self-selected and other-selected contingencies are equally effective in maintaining performance. Other studies have provided different results. For example, Dickerson and Creedon (1981) reported self-selected contingencies to be more effective than other-selected ones with second- and third-grade students in writing and math skills. Possible reasons for their results included the following:

(1) Children were given an unlimited range of contingencies instead of a set of choices from the experimenter; (2) Children in the self-selected contingencies group worked in groups of five and provided peer punishment for off-task or disturbing behavior; (3) The experimentor did not leave the room during the self-selection process; and (4) The selection of stringent self-selection contingencies was employed.

INSTRUCTIONAL IMPLICATIONS. Most of us prefer to select our own rewards when we are successful in achieving a goal. This is true whether the goal is in an academic area or in a more personal component of our lives. Sometimes we are unrealistic in selecting rewards, or the reward we desire is not available. In other instances the only possible rewards are under the control of someone else (e.g., teacher, parent). In these latter situations it may be necessary to use a reward that is selected by others. However, whenever possible, a self-monitoring system should provide self-selected contingencies.

Michele was a bright thirteen-year-old who had considerable experience with self-monitoring. Her current project was intended to improve her ability to work word problems in arithmetic. Initially, her reward was to have been thirty minutes of free time on Friday afternoon. This did not work very well, as Michele already had plenty of free time and had a tendency to get into trouble. Michele's arithmetic teacher questioned her about why the program was not working. Michele replied she wanted a reward that she could choose for herself, rather than having to depend entirely on the teacher, her parents, or her friends. The result was a change in the reward system. Michele could then earn points by successfully completing word problems. Points could be exhanged for bonus points on arithmetic tests, an increase in allowance, tickets to a local theatre, or free time at school. This new reward system gave Michele more freedom of choice and increased her personal responsibility for the program's success.

Self-Instruction

Some students can work independently to improve existing skills, while others lack this ability. Friedling and O'Leary (1979) reported that self-instructional training for mathematics, as well as general academics, has the greatest impact on skills already mastered. It also has a lesser impact on skills not being performed optimally. They further concluded that self-instructional training generalizes to tasks that are most similar to ones already known.

INSTRUCTIONAL IMPLICATIONS. Once a student has mastered the basic components of a relatively complex skill, the possibility for self-improvement is increased. For example, a student who learns to read or to do arithmetic at a rudimentary level can often improve reading or arithmetic computational speed on his or her own. Many programmed instructional materials, such as the Sullivan Reading Series, are based on this premise. Self-monitoring provides a useful tool for managing self-instruction.

> Cynthia wanted to increase her reading speed by 100 percent. She was already a fairly good reader, averaging nearly 250 words per minute with 80 percent comprehension. She decided she could use self-improvement training to accomplish her goal. She establsihed daily objectives of adding five words per minute to her overall speed. Her reasoning was that this would allow her to meet her goal in approximately 50 days. An 80 percent comprehension level was required at all times. Each day Cynthia was able to meet her goal, she gave herself five points in blue ink on a recording sheet. On days she surpassed her objective, she recorded the result in green ink. Deficit days were recorded in red ink. This gave her a good visual image of overall progress. If she met her overall goal, Cynthia promised herself to spend two weeks in the summer with her grandparents. If unsuccessful, she was going to forgo the purchase of any new records for three months. Cynthia finally met her goal in just thirty-seven days.

Conclusion

Self-monitoring is a viable technique for use with a wide range of general and specific academic behaviors. Investigators have reported that target behaviors such as staying on task, studying, and completing assignments can be improved with self-monitoring. The process is applied alone in some cases and along with rewards or punishments in others. The fact that general academic behaviors improve, however, does not automatically assure commensurate progress in more specific, nontargeted behaviors (e.g., mathematics, handwriting). This may be due to such factors as the ability of the student to use self-monitoring in a specific situation, ability of the student to retain new academic skills or to apply them in test-taking situations, inability of the teacher to take advantage of the student's self-monitoring skills, or a variety of other factors. These results parallel those found in the general behavior change literature (cf. Stokes & Baer, 1977). Despite the potential of self-monitoring to facilitate learning in a variety of academic functions, it is important for everyone concerned to remember the need to be flexible. Systems often have to be changed to meet the diverse needs of individuals. A self-monitoring program is no stronger than the people who design and implement it.

Chapter 6

INAPPROPRIATE CLASSROOM BEHAVIORS

Two areas of affective performance that have been improved with self-monitoring are disruption, aggression, and other inappropriate classroom problems traditionally identified by teachers, and personal behaviors that are typically more of a concern to the individual involved. The purpose of this chapter is to focus primarily on the former. Common examples include aggression toward peers, talking in class without permission, temper tantrums, and insubordination. The application of self-monitoring with personal functions (e.g., weight loss, anxiety, alcoholism, nail biting) is described in the next chapter, on covert and personal behaviors.

This chapter includes a general discussion of various strategies used to facilitate the use of self-monitoring with annoying classroom behaviors. The initial section is an introduction to appropriate intervention strategies. This is followed by a discussion of using self-ratings with disruptive students. Studies are cited in which student ratings are used alone. Next, the use of self-monitoring with aggression and emotional control problems is described, for both young children and adolescents. Emphasis is placed on the "turtle technique" with young children and systematic desensitization with older ones.

Introduction to Appropriate Interventions

Perhaps it would be useful to begin this section by describing three distinct groups of students identified in the self-monitoring literature on inappropriate classroom behaviors. First, a distinction should be made between disruptive and aggressive students. For example, a student who speaks out repeatedly in class without permission or who bangs loudly on the desk is *disruptive*. A student who picks a fight with a peer or who challenges the teacher's authority is *aggressive*. The disruptive student tends to focus on interrupting the instructional program, with or without including peers. The aggressive child, by definition, usually involves peers, whether they care to be involved or not. Typically, their preference is clearly not to be involved, as they are often the recipients of physical abuse. In some instances a child may be aggressive towards self as well (e.g., self-mutilator). A disruptive child may or may not be aggressive, but an aggressive child is almost always disruptive.

A third group of inappropriate classroom behaviors is exhibited by students who appear to be victims of their emotions. These individuals throw temper tantrums and are often provoked into fights by peers. Their behavioral pattern frequently leads to problems with authority figures. These students are frustrated with their absence of tolerance when placed under pressure and are sometimes referred to as *lacking emotional control*. Because of the manner in which the self-monitoring research has been organized, aggressive students and those that lack emotional control will be discussed concurrently.

Naturally, there are other types of inappropriate classroom behaviors in addition to the three described here. For example, there are overly shy or introverted children. Some exhibit extreme fears or even have specific phobias. Behaviors that are highly personal in nature are described in the next chapter. Traditional self-monitoring procedures discussed in the first half of the book can be used with all other behaviors, the vast majority of which are social.

Two general self-monitoring approaches are used to cope with disruptive students who may or may not also be aggressive. The simplest of these techniques is for the student to record the number of behaviors (e.g., talk-outs per period) or rate his or her behavior during a specific time interval (e.g., from one to five). Then the student is reinforced for self-monitored improvement. Since students may be inaccurate or exaggerate their scores when reinforcers are contingent upon them, some sort of teacher-checking system can be used. This approach is used with all students in the self-monitoring program initially. Later, teacher checking can occur at infrequent, random times. The technique is basically what Turkewitz, O'Leary, and Ironsmith (1975) used in their study, which is described in detail later in this chapter.

The second general method of self-monitoring is used with students who appear to be immature in controlling their emotions. These students may exhibit such behaviors as losing their temper, hitting other students or adults, throwing temper tantrums, and abusing animals or inanimate objects. These behaviors are quite common in toddlers, as parents of young children are keenly aware. Parents may ignore the tantrumlike behaviors of the toddler, which are likely to decrease gradually as children approach kindergarten age.

In most cases a slap on the hand, possibly combined with a loud "no," eventually decreases inappropriate hitting of animals and people. However, some students enter school with these immature behaviors. Teachers may find that simply ignoring some behaviors (e.g., temper tantrums) will eventually reduce them and that being sent to the principal's office may reduce others (e.g., swearing, hitting). When these simple techniques have been used over a period of days with no noticeable changes, other techniques can be employed. These techniques usually involve at least two of the following: (1) some form of relaxation training; (2) discussion and/or role playing of appropriate alternative behaviors; and (3) self-monitoring of the problem behavior and reinforcement for acceptable improvement.

Robin, Schneider, and Dolnick (1976) developed this type of program and successfully used it with primary students. They referred to their particular program as the "turtle technique." The technique is described in detail later in this chapter. A system developed by Wolpe (1976), called "systematic desensitization," can also be applied for the same kinds of problems in intermediate and secondary students. Systematic desensitization was initially developed for clinical use with clients who were experiencing debilitating fears (e.g., test anxiety, claustrophobia). Older students can be taught to use this technique with their aggressive responses.

Both the turtle technique and systematic desensitization should be used with students who wish to improve but who appear to exercise little control over their emotions or the behaviors that immediately follow emotional outbursts. These students are often described as "having a short fuse." Specific behavioral patterns resemble those described in the vignette in Chapter 1.

If a student is hitting peers, destroying objects, or exhibiting other aggressive behaviors while not also displaying visible signs of emotional distress (e.g., face turning red, voice being loud with audible breaks), another technique should be used. The social bully, for instance, would be a poor candidate for either the turtle technique or systematic desensitization. A more general type of self-monitoring might be preferred here, provided a reward can be identified that is more reinforcing than the superiority feelings derived from picking on others.

Self-Rating with Disruptive and Academic Performance

Turkewitz, O'Leary, and Ironsmith (1975) investigated eight students, aged seven to eleven years, with high rates of disruptive behaviors. These behaviors included inappropriate verbalizations, aggression, inattention, and being out of their seat at inappropriate times. Students were taught to self-evaluate their social and academic behaviors using a one-(poor)-to-five (excellent) scale. They initially self-evaluated both forms of behavior on a card taped to their desk. The card was similar to the one in Figure 6-1. At the same time, their teacher evaluated their behaviors without providing any consequences. A token system was then implemented based upon the teacher's evaluations of the two forms of behavior (i.e., social and academic). Points could be exchanged for extrinsic rewards.

The token system was gradually shifted to self-ratings. Students were told that if their ratings were within one point of teacher scores or matched teacher ratings, then they would actually earn the number of points they had given themselves. These points could be exchanged later for extrinsic rewards. A bonus point was also awarded for variations of one point or less. If a difference between teacher and student ratings exceeded one point, zero points were earned. Checking for agreement between teacher and student evaluations was reduced from 100 percent to 50 percent of the time. Later this checking, or matching of teacher and student ratings, was reduced even further to 33 1/3 percent of the time.

The matching approach (i.e., comparing student with teacher ratings) decreased disruptive behaviors more effectively than a comparable nonmatching evaluation based only on a teacher

		M	T	W	Th	F
Week 1	Disruptive (D) Academic (A)					
Week 2	Disruptive (D) Academic (A)					
Week 3	Disruptive (D) Academic (A)					
Week 4	Disruptive (D) Academic (A)					
Week 5	Disruptive (D) Academic (A)					

Instructions: Place a rating of 1 to 5 for both disruptive and academic behaviors. If you talk-out a lot in class, touch or hit your neighbor, or frequently leave your desk, give yourself a 1 under the day of the week in the "D" column. If you do not do these things at all, give yourself a 5. If you do them some but not very often, give yourself a 3. A 2 is used when you talk, hit, touch, or leave your desk only one or two times a day. A 4 is used when you pretty much misbehave, but not as much as when you have a really bad day. Use the 1 to 5 scale for doing your work in class, too. If you turn in all your work and it is neat and correct, give yourself a 5 in the "A" column under the day of the week. If you do most of your work and it is correct, give yourself a 4. A 3 is used for less work and a 2 for doing a little work. A 1 is for a really bad day when you did not do your work. Remember, I will check your work, and if we agree on your ratings, you can earn points. Otherwise, you can lose points.

Figure 6-1. A self-rating notecard for disruptive and academic behaviors.

evaluation token system. This finding indicates students perform better when they are personally involved in the monitoring process. In this particular study the matching condition was eventually withdrawn totally. The result was a small increase in disruptive behaviors. Then, extrinsic reinforcers for points earned were gradually withdrawn with one-half of the students, those whose names were not drawn from a box at the end of the day. Students whose names were drawn received extrinsic reinforcers for their points, while the others did not. Total fading of backup reinforcers was accomplished by subsequently withdrawing one-third of the names and then one-eighth of the names. Finally no names were withdrawn. Each reduction in extrinsic reinforcers led to a small increase in disruptive behavior. The overall behavior, however, remained between one-third and one-half of baseline levels.

Results indicated a matching system involving teacher and student ratings can lead to accurate self-ratings and improve disruptive behaviors. Improvements can also be enhanced when both parties participate in the evaluation process and when extrinsic rewards are introduced.

INSTRUCTIONAL IMPLICATIONS. The use of a matching system (e.g., the one suggested by Turkewitz) along with self-evaluation or self-recording appears to be promising for coping with disruptive behaviors. Teachers who use these two components will need to spend some time initially training students and making frequent matching checks. Later, however, the teacher becomes progressively less involved and should be able to expect continued low levels of disruptive behaviors.

> Clara was an eleven-year-old girl who was often subordinate to the teacher. Her mother reported she had been sassy with everyone for as long as she could remember. Clara's teacher decided to introduce Clara to self-monitoring, along with a program in which she could earn points for reducing derogatory statements. Points could then be exchanged for privileges. At first Clara used her self-monitoring program on her own. Progress was slow, as Clara often tended to cheat while recording results of her tally sheet. Her teacher then began to record behaviors along with Clara. Bonus points were awarded for accuracy. The frequency of insubordinate behaviors began to improve slightly. Accuracy, however, improved dramatically when Clara knew she was being carefully watched. Eventually, the

teacher added two incentives to the system. A week without progress would result in a call to Clara's mother, while a 30 percent or better improvement rate would mean an hour of free time in the gym on Friday afternoon. Significantly improved progress began to be noted beginning with the first week.

Self-Ratings Without Teacher Monitoring

Hall, Broden, and Mitts (1973) conducted a self-monitoring study in which self-rating was used exclusively without teacher participation. Their study focused on an eighth-grade boy with a problem of disruptive talk-outs during math class. His behavior was recorded using predetermined ten-second intervals. Audible and inaudible talk-outs (i.e., lips moving while facing another student) were included. On-task behavior and attention to teacher were also noted. Self-monitoring was done on a slip of paper with a line for his name and the date. A small square was used to tally each talk-out. At the top of the page were the simple instructions, "Put a mark down every time you talk-out."

Self-monitoring resulted in dramatic decreases in talk-outs when compared to baseline levels. When the class period was divided in half to make interclass comparisons, the positive effects of self-monitoring were again demonstrated.

After thirty days on the program, talk-outs were again increasing to levels as high as those noted during initial baseline. This finding indicates that the effects of self-monitoring without consequences or reactive effects may be limited over time. The most dramatic effects were observed during the initial twenty-five days. The investigators could have strengthened their study if they had introduced a matching component similar to the one used by Turkewitz et al.

INSTRUCTIONAL IMPLICATIONS. The Hall et al. self-monitoring technique is potentially viable for managing disruptive behavior. However, the effects of self-monitoring alone are only temporary. A contingency could be introduced after ten or so days, in which the student is rewarded for reducing intervals of disruptive behavior. Also, a matching technique may be necessary to assure that students do not exaggerate their improvements. This matching technique can be adapted from the Turkewitz et al. study.

Willie, a thirteen-year-old male, was often reprimanded for acting-out behaviors in class. He received considerable satisfaction from peers from being the "class clown." Willie's teacher was frustrated by his behavior and decided to try self-monitoring. The system was based on earning points by reducing off-task behaviors. Points were cumulative and could be exchanged at the end of class for an array of possible rewards. Willie worked at the program conscientiously. By the beginning of the second week, results began to diminish. Willie's behaviors soon reverted to their earlier level. The reason was that peer reinforcement was greater than any of the available rewards. The reward system was changed so that Willie could earn opportunities to peer tutor with his points. This lead to a reduction in his off-task behaviors to nearly zero per day.

Managing Aggression and Emotional Control Problems

Young Children, Aggression, and Emotional Control Problems

Self-management of aggression and emotional control problems by emotionally disturbed students was investigated by Robin, Schneider, and Dolnick (1976). The procedure they used was called the "turtle technique." Children were taught to pull their arms and legs in close to their body, put their heads on their desk, and imagine they were turtles withdrawing into their shell. They were told to respond in this way when about to encounter an aggressive situation or when frustrated and about to throw a tantrum. As might be expected, this approach probably has considerably more utility with younger students than older ones.

The turtle technique is an excellent example of antecedent control; that is, the student is attempting to influence a behavior that is expected to occur. Other behavior control strategies were also involved in the Robin et al. study. For example, social reinforcers such as teacher and peer praise were included. These rewards that follow a behavior are actually a type of consequence control. Furthermore, problem-solving techniques, which offered alternatives to aggressive behavior, and methods for inducing deep muscle relaxation (Jacobson, 1983) were taught to students.

A discussion of problem-solving alternatives when confronted with aggressive behaviors was considered an important element in the Robin et al. study. Key points in the discussion were emphasized in role-playing situations. Instruction focused on learning a variety of acceptable responses when faced with aggression or tantrums. Students were also taught to evaluate the possible consequences of each response. Aggression was defined as a forceful movement directed at either another person or an inanimate object, which included hitting, throwing, kicking, grabbing, or tearing objects in the immediate environment.

Students were taught that prior to responding in a threatening situation, they should withdraw into the turtle position, use the muscle relaxation techniques, and consider alternatives and their consequences. Peer praise, teacher praise, and extrinsic reinforcers were initially employed as consequences for behaving in this manner. Programmed teacher praise and extrinsic rewards were gradually faded. However, students may have continued to receive unplanned teacher and peer praise.

The turtle technique was initially taught in a game format. Whenever a peer or the teacher called out "turtle," students were expected to assume the described position. Later, this skill was transferred to frustrating or aggressive situations. For example, a peer or the teacher might say "turtle" when two children appeared on the verge of an emotional encounter.

A reduction in aggressive behaviors was noted in all eleven children who participated in the study. Results were validated by independent observers.

INSTRUCTIONAL IMPLICATIONS. The turtle technique is useful for younger students who lack control over their emotions, especially in frustrating situations. The technique may work best when used with a small group or the whole class at once, rather than individually. In this way peers can serve as reinforcing agents. Also, individual students are not singled out or stigmatized even though they may be among a small minority who are displaying inappropriate behaviors.

> Sammy was a seven-year-old with a history of quick-tempered responses. He worked well when left alone by classmates. The slightest provocation, however, tended

to result in an emotional, and often physical, response. He understood his behavior was inappropriate and likely to get him into trouble. Because of his interest in doing better, Sammy's teacher introduced the turtle technique. The entire class participated. Now, when Sammy is confronted with a possible social problem, he responds in a turtlelike manner and reviews his options. These include: (1) hitting the aggressor; (2) remaining inactive with head down until the problem has passed; (3) leaving the area without looking at the person; (4) calling on the teacher for assistance; (5) returning to work; or (6) entering into a discussion with the provoking person(s). By the time Sammy has had an opportunity to go into the turtle response and review his options, enough time has usually elapsed to calm his temper Sammy used a simple self-monitoring procedure to record his success rate. After each emotional encounter he rated his behavior from one to five, with one being an inappropriate response and five being an appropriate one. Each successful experience was followed by teacher praise. Weekly improvement resulted in a tangible reward (e.g., reduced homework for the weekend).

Managing Aggression and Emotional Control Problems in Adolescents

Adolescents undergo confusing and often extreme hormonal changes, as well as fluctuations in peer relations. Some appear to be children in the body of adults; others appear to be adults in the body of children; and still others can be either on a given day.

These hormonal changes may lead to poorly understood emotions and feelings. The influence of peers increases and often conflicts with values observed at home. Also, expectations exist for more mature behavior along with less adult supervision. Most individuals survive adolescence with problems that are relatively minor in nature, although they may not have seemed minor to the person at the time. A small minority, however, cannot adequately manage the combination of hormonal changes, peer influence, and decreased adult supervision.

One type of behavior often observed in these students is frequent fights. These students are the ones who rarely, if ever, initiate a fight. However, they are constantly drawn into them. They typically engage in both verbal and physical altercations. Again, these are not the school bullies but are often the target of bullies and peers in general. They are teased, harrassed, and provoked into verbally and physically aggressive responses. These reactions lead them into uncomfortable meetings with principals and teachers when emotions are still strong. This may result in unfortunate verbal and physical exchanges involving authority figures. These students clearly need to manage their emotions and to practice appropriate responses.

Wolpe (1976) developed a technique called "systematic desensitization." Its purpose is to help students manage emotional responses which have been making their lives difficult. The technique has been successful with a wide variety of fears, phobias, and other emotional problems (Yates, 1975).

An important component of systematic desensitization is muscle relaxation. Steps for achieving muscle relaxation are summarized below.

Bernstein and Borkovec (1973, p. 25) suggested the following general steps for each of the muscle group: (1) the individual's attention should be focused on the muscle group. (2) At a predetermined cue from the teacher, the muscle group is tensed. (3) Tension is maintained for a period of five to seven seconds. (4) At a predetermined cue, the muscle group is released. (5) The individual's attention is maintained upon the muscle group as it relaxes.

The muscle groups in order of progression are:

1. dominant hand and forearm
2. dominant biceps
3. nondominant hand and forearm
4. nondominant biceps
5. forehead
6. upper cheeks and nose
7. lower cheeks and jaws
8. neck and throat
9. chest, shoulders, and upper back
10. abdominal or stomach region
11. dominant thigh
12. dominant calf
13. dominant foot

14. nondominant thigh
15. nondominant calf
16. nondominant foot

Students can practice these steps in unemotional settings and later apply them in actual problem settings. The same approach can be used with the turtle technique by younger students. Similarly, students can practice role playing and discussion of possible alternatives in contrived situations. Then the students can use their skills in actual emotion-laden situations. Students can observe the effects of their responses on peers and rate the appropriateness of the responses. Finally, a reward system may be used to reinforce desirable improvements. Teachers may initially need to check for student accuracy in self-evaluation. Figure 6-2 is an example of a self-evaluation card a student might use.

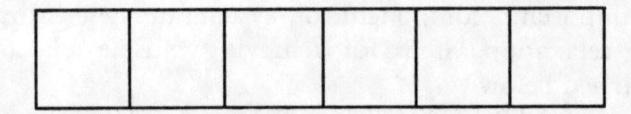

Instructions: Rate your behavior from one to five after you have been taunted or teased by someone. A five would be used for such behaviors as ignoring the student, walking away without saying anything, or changing the subject. A four would be used when you tease the student back and then walk away. A three would be used when calling the student a name. A two would be used for such behaviors as hitting or shoving the student. A one would be used for such responses as fighting and then talking back to an adult about it or using too loud a voice or foul language.

Figure 6-2. A self-rating chart for aggressive behavior.

Conclusion

The cited studies on self-monitoring disruptive classroom behaviors indicate that training students to record their performance may or may not be sufficient in itself as a therapeutic tool. However, pairing self-monitoring with a matching contingency to teacher-monitoring can be effective. Results indicate that this matching approach often leads to decreases in disruptive behaviors as compared to performance in teacher-controlled settings or when planned consequences are based entirely on self-monitoring. Reductions in disruptive behaviors without planned consequences tend to last for several weeks but in some cases begin to return to previous levels after a month or two. When self-monitoring effects continue beyond this point, it is probably due to a change in the classroom, planned or unplanned. That is, a child's ecosystem of reinforcers and punishers is altered in a favorable manner. For example, a student could begin to receive peer, teacher, or parental attention for new, more socially acceptable behaviors. Or, he or she could encounter fewer punishers for disruptive and less socially acceptable behaviors.

The Robin et al. study provides several techniques aimed at young children labeled impulsive or aggressive. The model of turtle-like behaviors (e.g., pulling arms and legs close to the body and placing heads on the desk) is probably well suited to children who have been read stories concerning animals. The use of a game format for teaching the technique, as well as teacher and peer praise, is probably important as well.

Transferring the turtle technique to an actual aggressive or frustrating situation might be difficult for some students due to the covert nature of the prevailing emotions. That is, students may initially feel the need to react emotionally rather than respond like a turtle. A teacher may need to identify precipitating situations and prompt some students by saying, "turtle." This prompt could eventually be faded as a student gains confidence.

Robin et al. also used deep muscle relaxation techniques that have enjoyed widespread use for several years. These techniques are helpful for reducing maladaptive emotions by alternatively tensing and relaxing large muscle groups. They are probably useful for people of all ages in a variety of stressful situations, as described in the section on adolescents.

Other strategies used by Robin et al. involved role playing and discussion of problem-solving alternatives when confronted with aggressive behaviors. These strategies are commonly used by counselors, teachers, and others who work with problem students. They are probably unnecessary with many children who are aware of possible alternatives and who occasionally employ them for short periods in the presence of powerful punishers (e.g., an authoritarian father).

Teachers are often reminded of behaviors they need to reinforce when they use role playing and when they discuss appropriate alternatives. These strategies might also create artificial occasions for teachers to reinforce appropriate behaviors that tend to occur infrequently (e.g., doing an unexpected favor for someone who has called you by an unflattering name).

Role playing and discussion of alternatives to aggressive behaviors are especially helpful with students who lack normal social development. These students often lack appropriate role models among their family or friends. They may also have failed to receive meaningful consequences during the times in which they have responded appropriately.

The use of self-monitoring and systematic desensitization for adolescents is a skill package that can be applied with a wide variety of problem behaviors. Students initially learn to relax and monitor their responses in frustrating situations. Later, they can apply these skills with other emotional problems, such as those discussed in the next chapter on personal and covert behaviors.

Chapter 7

PERSONAL AND COVERT BEHAVIORS

In the last chapter we reviewed the use of self-monitoring as it relates to inappropriate classroom behaviors. Many behaviors are more personal and covert in nature. These include weight control, alcohol consumption, cigarette smoking, fingernail biting, sexual performance, anxiety, and a wide range of other functions. The purpose of this chapter is to discuss the role of self-monitoring with these behaviors. The chapter includes an introduction to personal and covert behaviors, including a brief review of the self-monitoring movement, a summary of the advantages of self-monitoring for improving personal and covert behaviors, and a discussion of potential problems when self-monitoring these behaviors, including possible solutions.

An Introduction to Personal and Covert Behaviors

The vast majority of human behaviors are overt; that is, they can be observed by two or more persons. Other behaviors are not so easily observed. They are called "covert" and are often highly personal. Self-monitoring can be used to observe, record, and improve both overt and covert types of behaviors.

Covert behaviors include those that are private by nature (e.g., thoughts, fantasies, impulses) and those that are private by tradition (e.g., excretion, sleep habits). The area of sexual dysfunction is a good example of behaviors that are private by tradition (Lobitz & Lopiccolo, 1972). Specific studies in this covert area have examined orgasmic dysfunction (McMullen & Rosen, 1979), frigidity (Madsen & Ullman, 1967) and premature ejaculation (Lowe & Mikulas, 1975).

Some covert behaviors are also private by circumstance. These include responses that are potentially observable but occur when trained observers are usually absent (e.g., between classes, during lunch, before and after school hours). The individual producing the behavior is frequently the only consistently available potential observer.

The distinction between events that are private by nature and those that are private by tradition or circumstance is important for practical and theoretical reasons. Two primary groups of what may be loosely termed "behaviorists" have become involved in the research on self-monitoring and the broader topic of self-control or self-management. The more traditional group concerns itself only with behaviors that are observable. This group has been labeled "radical behaviorists" (Brigham, 1982a). It is concerned both with environmental variables that exert antecedent and consequent control over target behaviors and with potentially observable behaviors that may be overt but are private by tradition. The second group has been labeled "cognitive behavior modifiers" (Meichenbaum, 1977). It has viewed unobservable events such as impulses, thoughts, and beliefs to be possible target behaviors, while also employing antecedent and consequent control over these and other, more overt behaviors. This position is in direct contradiction to Skinner (1953) in terms of what actually constitutes a "behavior." The focal point of discussion between these two groups may lie in a misinterpretation of Skinner about self-control. The debate is beyond the scope of this book, and the reader is referred to Brigham (1982a) for a more complete discussion.

Many of the studies we have discussed included accuracy checks by independent observers. This was possible because the behaviors were highly visible to relatively large numbers of people. In contrast, personal and covert behaviors are rarely, if ever, formally observed by observers. When independent observation does occur, it tends to influence or contaminate the target behavior. This contamination is referred to as *reactivity*, a term that we have used throughout the book.

Reactivity is often a significant factor, regardless whether a target behavior is overt or covert. However, the nature of most private behaviors may make them extremely susceptible to reactivity. When it is obvious that a particular behavior might be altered considerably by external observation, self-monitoring could be the most reasonable means of data collection (Ciminero, Nelson, & Lipinski, 1977). Reactivity tends to occur frequently with private behaviors that can be observed by an external party. It is also common with behaviors that are relatively easy to change (Peacock, Layman, & Richard, 1978).

INSTRUCTIONAL IMPLICATIONS. There are many types of personal and covert behaviors. Each must be analyzed in light of its peculiar characteristics before self-monitoring can be effectively used. For example, some personal behaviors can be verified by observation (e.g., sexual performance, weight loss). Others are far more susceptible to interpretation (e.g., thoughts, impulses, fantasies). In some instances reactivity is a major consideration, and self-observation is the only practical means of data collection.

> Wayne had trouble with sleep apnea, a condition in which he would literally stop breathing during sleep for periods of twenty to thirty seconds. As part of a treatment program, his doctor suggested that he tape-record the sounds that he made while sleeping. Then he and his doctor could listen to his breathing patterns and have a keener appreciation of his problem.

Self-recording of breathing patterns during sleep is actually a form of self-monitoring. If the observation had to be done by a second party, the reactive effect might serve to keep the individual awake or at least alter his sleep behavior.

The need to self-analyze and control private behavior in humans has been discussed for several decades (cf. Tolman, 1948). The issue did not come into prominence, however, until Homme (1965) published a well-known study on controlling covert acts with self-rewards. Numerous studies followed Homme's model (or a variation of it) during the late 1960s and early 1970s by cognitive behavior modifiers (Johnson, 1971; Mahoney, 1971; Todd, 1972, Tooley & Pratt, 1967). Meichenbaum (1974) eventually added a new element to self-control of covert behaviors by introducing the previously mentioned concept of self-instruction. That is, an individual can learn to improve a target behavior, often covert in nature, by verbally repeating to himself or herself a desired response. Self-instruction, when viewed in strictly observable terms, involves the teacher saying the steps and the student repeating them.

In the mid to late 1970s attention began to be focused on the use of self-management with depression (Anton, Dunbar, & Friedman, 1967; Lewinsohn & Talkington, 1979; Lewinsohn, Biglan, & Zeiss, 1976; Rush, Beck, Kovacs, & Hollon, 1977; Tharp, Watson, & Daya, 1974). More recent studies using self-management have examined unassertive individuals (Alden, Safran, & Weideman, 1979), common fears (Barrios & Shigetomi, 1980), test anxiety (Fremouw & Zitter, 1978), and interpersonal anxiety (Kanter & Goldfried, 1979). The wide range of covert behaviors that have been treated with self-monitoring supports the contention that the process is highly versatile.

Self-monitoring, when used with some personal and covert behaviors, evidences distinct similarities to systematic desensitization (Wolpe, 1961; 1973; 1976). Behaviors targeted for behavior change (e.g., fears, anxieties) and techniques of change (e.g., imagery) are common to both techniques. The relative importance of using various techniques in conjunction with systematic desensitization is not well understood. The desensitization procedure itself, however, can be quite effective (Yates, 1975).

Advantages of Self-Monitoring Personal and Covert Behaviors

A primary advantage of self-monitoring with personal and covert behaviors is the privacy it affords. For example, many individuals have a history of repeated failures. Others would merely like to improve their performance. Both groups might prefer to function without fear of ridicule, ostracism, or other aversive reactions if their performance fails to meet preconceived expectations. Self-monitoring provides them with an opportunity to improve many personal behaviors without fear of external review.

There are many additional advantages to self-monitoring personal and covert behaviors. Some of the more pertinent ones are discussed below.

Provides an Avenue for Improving Some Private Behaviors

Some teachers may have difficulty designing intervention strategies for certain private behaviors. The choice of therapeutic techniques may be limited. Self-monitoring provides an avenue for a student to assist the teacher and to work on his or her problem with minimum intrusions.

Stresses the Student's Role as a Primary Change Agent

When self-monitoring personal or covert behaviors, a student may be the only person who is aware that a behavior occurs or that it may be changing. This phenomenon places considerable emphasis on the student as a key member of the educational team. Responsibility of this type could contribute to greater self-reliance and esteem.

Allows Generalizations Back to Overt Behaviors

Self-monitoring skills learned through experience with covert behaviors may be generalized to overt functions. In fact, once a student becomes reasonably proficient with covert behaviors, the transfer back to more observable behaviors could be relatively simple. Conversely, self-monitoring of overt behaviors may be a preparatory step to employing the skill with covert behaviors.

Behaviors learned as a result of self-monitoring—either overt or covert—can be maintained over time (Turkewitz, O'Leary, & Ironsmith, 1973). This phenomenon is important because it allows both teachers and students to proceed to other important behaviors, with some assurance that improvements will last.

In addition to the advantages already cited, self-monitoring also allows: (1) generalizations to nonschool environments; (2) the teacher to have more free time for other tasks; and (3) an opportunity to improve a wide range of behaviors. These three advantages apply to both overt and covert events.

INSTRUCTIONAL IMPLICATIONS. Self-monitoring offers many advantages in addition to improving a target behavior. These advantages are often not apparent until desired changes in the behavior begin to occur. In addition to their obvious value, they also serve to reinforce the self-monitoring program and all associated benefits.

> Clara had always been reluctant to talk about her weight problem, particularly with peers who often made fun of her. She recognized the need to lose weight and

finally decided to talk about it with her school counselor. The counselor suggested a self-monitoring program in which only Clara would know the results. If the program worked, fine; if it did not, then only Clara would know. As Clara began to lose weight, her entire attitude began to change. She started to perform better in her classes, and her relationship with peers began to improve as well. When friends asked Clara how she did it, Clara merely smiled and thought about her self-monitoring program.

Potential Problems and Possible Solutions

It is relatively easy to measure changes that occur in highly visible behaviors. These include many changes in physical and cognitive domains. Examples include a ten-pound increase in body weight and a 40 percent increase in reading comprehension, respectively. Behavioral changes are usually not as apparent in covert functions. This is particularly true for behaviors that are covert by nature and/or that occur in the affective domain. For example, a girl's feelings toward her boyfriend may increase in intensity, but the degree of change is not as measurable. This phenomenon tends to limit quantifiable assessment, even though the girl may readily admit a change has occurred.

It is normally advisable to teach self-monitoring of overt behaviors before introducing covert ones. A primary reason is that overt events are generally more observable. This allows a teacher to make reliability checks during the instructional process to determine how well a student is acquiring self-monitoring skills. At least the teacher and student can compare notes to determine how accurate the latter is in making his or her counts. Reliability checks are particularly important with students who have an inaccurate perception of their behavior or fail to understand the relationship between their behavior and the behavior of peers (or adults). High levels of reliability, however, may not be crucial for improving behavior in many cases (Rosenbaum & Drabman, 1979).

Once behaviors private by tradition are introduced for use with self-monitoring, reliability checks usually become more difficult.

In fact, reliability checks involving behaviors that are covert by nature may be impossible. In many instances, the individual may be the only person to actually know if improvement is occurring. Honesty with self is of crucial importance. The need for self-determination may provide an unusual opportunity for some students, particularly those accustomed to a structured environment largely controlled by others.

As mentioned earlier, reactivity is often a useful phenomenon in the self-monitoring process. This is particularly true for overt behaviors. However, the effect of reactivity on covert behaviors may be difficult, if not impossible, to measure accurately. This does not imply that reactivity does not occur with covert behaviors; only that it is difficult to observe and is often not subject to reliability checks. Furthermore, its effect can be either positive or negative, although most studies indicate that if reactivity occurs, it is usually in the desired direction (Rosenbaum & Drabman, 1979).

The purpose of this section is to identify potential problems that may arise when students use self-monitoring with covert behaviors. Specific problems relate to defining measurable behaviors, coping with less conscious covert behaviors, and selecting a proper recording form. In addition to identifying potential problems, possible solutions are suggested.

Defining Measurement of Covert Behaviors

Designing a self-monitoring program for a covert behavior may be confusing. A desirable goal is to define the behavior operationally, in a way it can be easily measured. The measurement may need to consist of observable aspects of the actual behavior. For example, a girl's feelings toward her boyfriend are difficult to assess. Even she may have a difficult time defining them. However, she can measure the effects of her improved attitude. For example, she may now be seeing him an average of three hours a day as opposed to two hours a day in the past. She may also notice an increase in the number of minutes they spend on the telephone per week. Or, she may observe a decrease in the number of disagreements per month they experience. These overt aspects associated with covert behaviors may be more practical for purposes of observation.

Coping with Less Conscious Covert Behaviors

Not all personal or covert behaviors involve internal emotions or feelings. Some are actually observable, but the person is unaware they are occurring. These behaviors are borderline overt/covert and are included here because of their covert characteristics. A good example is a child's humming in class while she works. The behavior does not bother her; in fact, she may not even be aware of it. Her classmates and teacher, however, may be very disturbed.

Behaviors of this nature present unique self-monitoring problems because the person does not know what to count or record. There are several possible ways to cope with this problem. The first is to ask a friend to point out the behavior. This works reasonably well if the friend is present when the behavior occurs. For example, a person who speaks too loudly or too softly in normal conversations might use this strategy.

It might be awkward or embarrassing to have certain behaviors identified in social situations. For example, what if a person desired to count the number of times he burped, or the times he used the phrase "you know . . .?" In these instances, it might be preferable to use a portable audio cassette recorder. The behavior tally can be recorded on a checksheet or rating scale at a later time.

A related option is to ask a peer to remind a student of the behavior after the social situation has changed and the two individuals are the only ones present. It might also be a good idea to change the way in which the peer reports the behavior. For example, in a conversation occurring between a student and two peers, one peer's job could be to remind the student of the times he talks to someone without direct eye contact. Rather than inform him in front of a third party, which might be embarrassing, the preferred approach could be for the peer to address the student by his given name. Only the two parties would know the behavior had been noted. Self-monitoring should not be socially embarrassing. If it is, the system should be changed.

In some instances, a particular approach might be embarrassing only to the person involved. A reward system might be helpful in this regard. For example, an adolescent girl might feel awkward about her unconscious use of profanity. Keeping records might only make her feel worse because it focuses attention on the problem. She could deal with the problem by rewarding herself each day with a call to her boyfriend if she diligently records the number of inappropriate verbalizations. Her approach could be to ask a friend to turn on a pocket cassette recorder at designated fifteen-minute intervals during social situations. She could then listen to the tapes at night and tally the results.

Another alternative for recording some types of less conscious behaviors is to use a wristwatch with an alarm. The alarm can be set to sound at designated intervals (e.g., every thirty minutes). The person simply notices if the behavior is occurring at the time of the beep. Examples of behaviors that can be monitored in this way include cracking one's knuckles, grinding one's teeth, and twisting one's hair around a fingertip.

Some individuals use negative practice to overcome difficulties with monitoring unconscious behaviors. Negative practices can be useful with a variety of unconscious behaviors, including those that occur during sleep (e.g., tossing and turning, snoring, bedwetting). Negative practice means the person consciously forces himself or herself to perform the target behavior (e.g., nail biting). By paying attention during the behavior, the person also increases the likelihood of noticing the behavior when it occurs naturally. A key for effective negative practice (and thus, self-monitoring) is for the person to totally concentrate during practice sessions.

Selecting a Proper Recording Device

Another potential problem with respect to measuring personal and covert behavior involves the recording device. Many recording instruments are merely tabulations or simple checksheets. With covert behaviors, it may be preferable to use a rating scale or record a pair of behaviors rather than use a single checksheet. The difference is that rating scales allow evaluation of *degree*. The multiple behaviors indicate responses that should be increased as well as decreased. Checksheets only indicate yes or no. A rating scale, or recording a pair of behaviors, or tallying several forms about one behavior allows a student to evaluate a response within the range of two extreme polars. That is, one behavior is on one end of the scale, and its opposite is on the other. For example, one end might represent extreme social interaction and the other total isolation.

When a child uses a rating scale to record personal or covert behaviors, it is sometimes advisable initially not to view the baseline as it develops. This is especially true when an impressive graphic display is used. The reason is that the child could allow himself or herself to be influenced by a negative trend. That is, the observable trend could have a reactive effect on overall emotional adjustment.

INSTRUCTIONAL IMPLICATIONS. Every self-monitoring program, regardless of how simple, has potential pitfalls. This is particularly true with personal and covert behaviors because it is difficult to confirm accuracy through reliability checks. When a problem does occur, it is important to analyze it in an honest manner and decide on a possible solution. Often, a simple redefinition of the target behavior, or a change in how it is recorded, is all that is needed. The key is to be flexible and patient. It also helps to understand that the procedures will usually work, if given adequate opportunity.

> Danielle was a young adolescent who knew her attitude toward school needed considerable improvement. She became increasingly depressed as she reviewed her daily chart while recording baseline data over a two-week period. Soon she felt bad about two things, her attitude toward school and her poor chart. It would have been better if she had recorded each day's attitude on a separate piece of paper, dated it, and dropped it in a sealed shoe box. Then, at the end of the baseline period, she could have then recorded it all at once. Her intervention strategy could have been started immediately, thus counteracting her negativism.

> Randy was a male student who had problems with depression. He went to counseling and decided to use a self-monitoring program. Immediately, he experienced difficulty measuring his degree of emotional depression. He had initially decided to record the average number of minutes he spent alone per day for a two-week period. After trying this approach, he became discour-

aged because he was not sure how to define *alone*. Did sleeping hours count? What about the time he would have liked to spend with others but found himself alone due to circumstances (e.g., when driving to school)? When it is obvious that a mistake has been made in defining a behavior, his counselor reminded him, it is especially important to be flexible. Furthermore, Randy was told that when it is unclear as to what constitutes a viable measurement, it is often advisable to revise the operational definition. A behavior can be redefined and a new baseline begun. In Randy's case, he decided to count only the number of minutes of waking time in which he was alone and in which there was an opportunity to be with others. Another possible option he considered was to change his approach altogether and to monitor the time he spent in socialized activities.

Conclusion

The potential of self-monitoring with personal and covert behaviors has been formally recognized for several years (Homme, 1965), although the vast majority of research has focused on overt performance. This overt emphasis has only begun to change during the past decade to include expansion into private domains. More study is needed, however, if optimum results are to be achieved in the personal and covert areas. Potential areas of exploration include: (1) reviewing implications of self-monitoring for specific types of personal and covert behaviors (e.g., anxiety, depression); (2) reviewing the efficacy of various strategies for teaching self-monitoring techniques to both nonhandicapped and handicapped populations; (3) determining the relative value of various recording devices as they relate to personal and covert functions; (4) refining procedures for best defining personal and covert responses in operational terms; and (5) identifying new techniques for measuring and improving personal and covert behaviors.

We have examined the use of self-monitoring with academic behaviors, inappropriate classroom behaviors, and personal and covert behaviors. Two other areas that have appeared in the self-monitoring literature include vocational and self-help skills. We will discuss these topics next.

―――――――――――――― *Chapter 8* ――――――――――――――

VOCATIONAL AND SELF-HELP SKILLS

T he purpose of this chapter is to discuss the use of self-monitoring with vocational and self-help skills. These skills have utility with a variety of students, including adolescents in vocational education programs and young children who are learning to care for themselves. In addition, vocational and self-help skills are important elements in the curriculum of many handicapped students.

Our discussions are based on the available self-monitoring literature that relates to vocational and self-help skills. Unfortunately, the research that has been done in these areas is relatively limited. Despite this limitation, we have identified two pertinent studies that have implications for teaching these important skills via self-monitoring. Both of these studies were done with handicapped populations. Because investigators in both cases were highly successful in their use of self-monitoring, it is considered likely that their procedures would work equally well, if not better, with nonhandicapped populations.

One study we will review used self-monitoring among institutionalized, delinquent girls who have not responded satisfactorily to the regular token economy system. The other study employed monitoring with retarded adults to teach self-care skills (i.e., self-showering and clothing and wardrobe maintenance). In each case, the methods used can be applied with little or no adaptation to other populations.

Many employers, vocational counselors, and other individuals are concerned with increasing work productivity. An especially interesting part of the vocational study by Seymour and Stokes (1974) is the teaching of students to increase the praise they receive from staff. In some respects this may be as important as actual work habits because of the reinforcement it provides. In the long term this incentive may result in greater job satisfaction, improved staff morale, and increased productivity. Increased staff praise may be especially useful when placing a student in a work setting in which co-workers are biased toward the individual. For example, a bias may be due to such factors as a student's age, a history of delinquency, or a label such as *mental retardation*.

The second study, by Matson, Marchetti, and Adkins (1980), was designed to teach showering and wardrobe maintenance. Showering was taught in twenty-nine steps and included such items as putting out one's towel and washcloth, washing specific body part, putting dirty clothes in a hamper, and applying deodorant. A similar set of eighteen steps was involved in the program for clothing and wardrobe maintenance. These steps included hanging shirts, pants, or dresses, folding undergarments, and placing each item in its respective place. Parents and dormitory personnel are often interested in teaching these types of skills to both handicapped and nonhandicapped youngsters. The involvement of children in the monitoring/teaching process appears to increase the effectiveness of the procedure. It can also decrease parent or dorm personnel time demands. A vignette has been included with each study as an example of how specific adaptions can be made in order to use the research procedures in practical situations.

Vocational Skills

Seymour and Stokes (1976) used self-monitoring to improve work skills in a residential vocational center. Their study involved four adolescent girls who had not responded satisfactorily to the staff-monitored token economy system. One of the primary purposes was to cue staff members to increase their use of verbal praise. The girls were aged fourteen to eighteen and had IQs of 68, 76, 96, and 104. The staff allowed girls to earn tokens for vocational, social, and self-care behaviors, while losing them for inappropriate behaviors. Tokens could be exchanged for activities, privileges, and articles (e.g., candy, cigarettes, clothing, cosmetics). The four girls were selected to participate in the self-monitoring research program because they had not responded to the standard token economy.

Self-monitoring was initially applied to work behaviors in four settings: the classroom, workshop, office, and kitchen. A therapist introduced self-monitoring to the girls, explaining that they needed to work efficiently and avoid conflicts in order to succeed later in school or in work settings outside the institution. Appropriate work behaviors were discussed and written on note cards (Figure 8-1). Two of the girls used three-minute intervals for recording. The other two girls could not tell time and so used event or permanent product recording (e.g., direction "B" in Figure 8-1).

(front)　　　　　　　work behaviors include:

        1. looking at work
        2. doing the work set and not something else
        3. not fiddling
        4. when getting something
        5. not dawdling
  and 6. not talking out of place

(back)　　Instructions: (A) Put the first letter of your name when working throughout three-minute intervals, or (B) put the first letter of your name upon making five bags or completing five jobs in the kitchen. Put the same letter a second time when you cue the staff for praise.

Classroom	Workshop	Office	Kitchen

Figure 8-1. Self-monitoring cards for work and cueing behaviors using internals and permanent products (Seymour and Stokes, 1976).

The girls received one token for each two marks on their cards. At first, tokens were delivered at the end of each classroom or workshop session. Later, all tokens were given at the end of the day. Cheating was checked by an independent observer at least once every three days. A penalty of ten tokens was imposed for cheating.

Work behaviors were self-monitored by each girl in the various work sites (e.g., kitchen, workshop). The procedure produced an independently measured increase in percentage of work behavior for each girl in each of the four settings. In addition, the average rate of staff praise increased as the rate of independently assessed cueing increased. Cueing was apparently necessary to evoke staff praise.

Self-recording cues were introduced next by the therapist. This was done by telling the girls that staff workers had not responded to improvement in their work. Girls were instructed to point to their improvements by using cues. Cues included such statements as "Am I working well?" "Look at how much work I've done," or "How's this, Miss . . . ?" (p. 44). These cues were discussed and observed via role playing. The girls were also asked not to reveal that they were cueing for praise. Cueing was to occur at completion of an article of work or at the end of a class period when a staff member was nearby. Cues were self-monitored and recorded on notecards; that is, girls marked the first letter of their name in a space next to the one where work behaviors were tallied. A token was given for each cue recorded by the student. Tokens were also delivered for appropriate work behaviors.

Average rate of staff praise actually dropped during the period in which only work behaviors were self-monitored. Work behaviors, however, increased in all categories during both work and cueing phases.

Later, tokens were withdrawn in short follow-up investigations to determine if increased staff praise might continue and maintain the levels of work and cueing behavior. When the tokens were withdrawn, work behavior continued at the high levels. Cueing and staff praise dropped slightly but were maintained near the prior levels when tokens were used.

The follow-up studies lasted for only a week, and results need to be interpreted with caution. Whether the girls would continue their working, cueing, and self-monitoring behaviors when only the staff praise was used as reinforcers is not clear. They might also continue to use the self-recording due to the greater number of tokens they were likely to earn when returned to the regular token system.

INSTRUCTIONAL IMPLICATIONS: The Seymour and Stokes study illustrates several important elements in a successful self-monitoring program. These elements include: (1) the value of combining a positive reinforcer (i.e, tokens) with a punisher (i.e., loss of tokens); (2) the role of both an independent observer and token penalty to encourage accurate counts; (3) the simplicity and practicality of simple notecard recording; and (4) the probability of maintaining newly learned behaviors, especially when reinforcers are present. The same practices can be used to improve a wide range of behaviors in individuals of all ages and ability levels. Their practicality is not limited to vocational skills or to delinquent girls.

Self-monitoring can be applied to both job performance (e.g., number of bricks layed per hour, quality of repaired fender, plant-growing skills) and work habits (e.g., getting to work on time, displaying proper manners and respect for superiors). For maximum success it is important to identify specifically the skill that needs improving and to follow the basic self-monitoring procedures described in Chapter 3.

> Mr. Robertson was a teacher in the vocational wing of a comprehensive high school. He taught automobile repair. He also encouraged his students to be hard-working and conscientious. The students enjoyed occasional attention from their other teachers, but Mr. Robertson felt that several of them rarely received the praise they deserved. This was especially true for his students from special education classes, many of whom had frequently failed in academics but who performed well in his class. He decided to teach his students a simple cueing procedure to see if he could increase the number of times they were rewarded (by praise or otherwise). Each time a teacher walked nearby as they were working, the students were instructed to ask him or her to check their work. Furthermore, each would politely express appreci-

ation for positive remarks. They would also record each positive remark on a notecard. Students were praised an average of three times daily. After the procedure was initiated, the praise rate climbed to an average of eleven times a day. Later, when the cueing and monitoring were faded, the average declined to six times daily. Mr. Robertson was still satisfied, however, as his students were now receiving twice as much positive attention as they had been.

Self-Help Skills

Matson, Marchetti, and Adkins (1980) worked with institutionalized, moderately retarded adults. They used self-evaluation and self-monitoring to increase one of two self-help behaviors. The two target behaviors were showering and wardrobe maintenance (e.g., hanging, folding, and storing clothes appropriately). Each behavior was actually a set of simple, sequential responses. For example, showering was divided into the following twenty-nine steps. This procedure is called a task-analytic approach to teaching.

1. Place towel and washcloth on stand beside shower.
2. Turn on water faucet.
3. Adjust the temperature.
4. Step under the water until the body is wet.
5. Lather cloth with soap and place soap in tray.
6. Wash face with cloth.
7. Wash left arm with cloth.
8. Wash under left arm with cloth.
9. Wash right arm with cloth.
10. Wash under right arm with cloth.
11. Wash chest and stomach with cloth.
12. Wash genital area with cloth.
13. Wash buttock with cloth.
14. Wash left leg with cloth.
15. Wash right leg with cloth.
16. Rinse off and wring out washcloth.
17. Rinse off soap and turn off water.
18. Get towel.

19. Dry face.
20. Dry arms.
21. Dry remainder of body.
22. Dry chest and stomach.
23. Dry genital area.
24. Dry back.
25. Dry buttocks.
26. Dry right leg.
27. Dry left leg.
28. Put towel and cloth in dirty-clothes hamper.
29. Apply deodorant to underarms. (P. 491)

Wardrobe maintenance was organized in less sequential order and was actually more of a list. Specific behaviors included:
1. Shirt hung neatly
2. Pants hung neatly
3. Dresses hung neatly
4. Out-of-season shirts folded and stored neatly
5. Out-of-season dresses folded and stored neatly
6. Out-of-season pants folded and stored neatly
7. No inappropriate clothing in wardrobe (e.g., underclothes)
8. No inappropriate items in wardrobe (e.g., food)
9. No dirty clothes in wardrobe
10. Shoes in bottom of wardrobe, placed side-by-side
11. Underwear neatly folded
12. T-shirts or slips neatly folded
13. Pajamas folded in nightstand or under pillow
14. Socks or hose in nightstand in an orderly fashion
15. No inappropriate items in nightstand
16. No inappropriate clothing in nightstand (e.g., pants, shoes)
17. No dirty clothes in nightstand
18. Items placed on nightstand in an orderly fashion (P. 491)

An arbitrary criterion for use by independent raters for task completion of skills was eighteen out of twenty-nine for showering and fifteen out of eighteen for wardrobe maintenance. Also, each step was self-recorded when completed to allow a more sensitive measure of percentage of steps done successfully.

The investigators compared the results of a standard treatment group with those of the retarded adults. The standard treatment group used the techniques most commonly cited in the literature for teaching self-help behaviors. Specific techniques included: (1) verbal prompts (e.g., "Now, you wash your arms"); (2) modeling (e.g., "Fold your shirts like this"); (3) manual guidance (i.e., kinesthetically moving through the steps); (4) social reinforcement for correct performance; (5) shaping until the target behavior itself was performed; (6) fading (i.e., gradually eliminating prompts); and (7) chaining, or linking small bits of behavior into complete steps (e.g., "First, put the hanger through the arm holes; then, button the button").

The retarded adults followed this same format during the week but used the additional features of self-evaluation and self-recording on Friday. They were asked to evaluate their performance in showering or in wardrobe maintenance for the previous week. Subjects could choose the target behavior they preferred to improve. They were asked if they had done good, bad, or okay, or if they deserved special recognition. Social reinforcement was programmed for adults whose responses were in agreement with independent raters, regardless of actual performance.

If progress did not occur, subjects were asked to state a reason. Suggestions for doing better next week were also solicited. Appropriate suggestions were praised. When suggestions were not made, the trainer identified specific ideas, which were then repeated by the adult.

A chart was used to self-monitor improvement. When subjects achieved more steps than they had in the previous week, they were allowed to place a star on their chart. A verbal explanation of their improvement was also written on the chart by the trainer.

Actual improvements, as well as self-evaluation accuracy, were major purposes of the study. The idea was to use self-evaluation and self-recording to achieve these purposes. Several staff members (trainers) delivered social praise for improvement in a programmed manner. Comments from the retarded adults indicated that they enjoyed the increased attention and placing of stars on their charts for desired improvements.

The research group of retarded adults improved in their behaviors dramatically compared to the standard treatment group that did not use self-evaluation or self-recording or receive social praise. The standard treatment group improved less than 10 percent of their prior success rate. The research group increased over 15 percent using the same list of behaviors. The difference could be due to self-evaluation and self-recording and/or to the increased social attention. It could also be attributed to some other aspect of the procedure (e.g., increased staff acceptance of involving residents in the treatment program).

INSTRUCTIONAL IMPLICATIONS: Self-help skills include several functions related to caring for ourselves. These include feeding, combing hair, brushing teeth, toileting, bathing, and general hygiene. The Matson et al. study focused on two of these skills, showering and wardrobe maintenance. The procedures they used can be applied to other self-help behaviors.

Basic procedures used by Matson et al. included task analysis, verbal prompts, modeling, manual guidance, social praise, fading, and forward chaining. The investigators also added self-evaluation and self-recording with the experimental group. Each of these procedures is well known among behavior modification specialists. Furthermore, each procedure can easily be combined with self-monitoring.

When using task analysis, it is important to divide each skill into its simplest elements. This is especially crucial for retarded students and young children. For example, feeding oneself is actually a combination of six distinct skills; blowing, sucking, chewing, swallowing, tongue control, and lip movement. Therefore, self-monitoring would probably not focus on feeding per se but on each of its component parts. Ideally, these parts would be taught one at a time and then integrated into the more complex behavior.

Two vignettes are provided below to illustrate the practicality of using self-monitoring with self-help skills. The first applies to young children in a home setting and the second to a group of elderly persons in a nursing home.

> Linda was a mother of two young sons who left her home in a constant state of clutter. This was particularly true of the bedroom and bathroom. Articles of clothing, toys, and collections of every sort, some alive and some long since passed away, were strewn across the house in

general and the two rooms in particular. Items were frequently discovered, often from their odor, under beds, chairs, and sofa. Linda decided to put a list of behaviors to be accomplished on the boys' bedroom wall. The list included: (1) Put all dirty clothes in the hamper; (2) Put all animals, alive and dead, outside; (3) Put all toys in the toy box; (4) Put all muddy shoes on the porch; and (5) Put all food items in the refrigerator or the trash. The boys were expected to meet all five criteria by 7:00 PM each night of the week and 8:00 PM on weekends. The boys' allowance was dependent upon successfully completing the items. Each evening Linda would observe the bedroom and bathroom and check items on the list that had been successfully completed. The boys' maximum allowance was seventy cents a week; that is, they could earn ten cents each for the days in which all five criteria were met. Eventually, they began to earn their full allowance on a regular basis. At that point Linda let them put their own marks on the wall list, while occasionally checking for accuracy.

Mary did volunteer work in a nursing home for elderly persons. Many residents were unable to feed themselves. She decided to use self-monitoring to improve self-feeding skills. Mary designed a large chart with each resident's name and a checking area for each successful self-feeding. A special snack was provided to each resident on Friday afternoon if improvement was noted over the prior week. Each resident was responsible for keeping track of his or her own performance. Staff were asked to praise each resident who actively participated, whether they were successful in a given meal or not. Over a three-week period, an overall improvement of 27 percent was noted. Because of the increased interest in self-feeding, the professional staff began a structured training program using a task-analytic, self-monitoring approach.

Conclusion

Self-monitoring has consistently been demonstrated to have utility for teaching a wide variety of skills. In this chapter we have focused on two types of skills, vocational and self-help on which relatively little research has been done. The studies that have been done use well-defined self-monitoring procedures that can be easily generalized to other behaviors.

Perhaps it is ironic that the only existing research on self-monitoring in the areas of vocational and self-help skills has been done with delinquent and retarded populations, respectively. These are certainly important areas in which additional self-monitoring research is warranted. It is probably reasonable to conclude that if self-monitoring can be successful with students who are traditionally considered hard to reach, then it can also be used with nonhandicapped persons.

In the past four chapters we have discussed a variety of self-monitoring studies. These studies have related to academic performance, classroom behaviors, personal and covert functions, and vocational and self-help skills. These general topics were selected not only because of their importance in our daily lives but because existing research has focused on them. Other areas of our lives might be identified that are important as well. Our intent has not been to apply self-monitoring to every type of human behavior. Rather, we have attempted to demonstrate the overall practicality of self-monitoring, the fact that it has utility across a broad range of routine functions.

In the last chapter we will make an effort to summarize the practical aspects of self-monitoring. That is, we hope to integrate the procedural elements described in Chapters 1 through 4 with the research conclusions drawn from Chapters 5 through 8.

Chapter 9

SELF-MANAGEMENT: THE COMPLETED PROCESS

As students mature they are capable of assuming increased responsibility for self-monitoring. Once their skills become relatively well developed, they can even carry the process one step further to include *self-management*. The purpose of this chapter is to provide a synopsis of the self-management concept, a review of the *ABC*s of behavior change, a description of two divergent schools of self-management, and suggestions for teaching self-management skills to students.

Self-monitoring is used primarily to observe, evaluate, monitor, or record behavior. With self-management, students also learn to arrange antecedents (i.e., stimuli that occur prior to a behavior) and consequences (e.g., stimuli that occur immediately following a behavior) to increase desirable and decrease undesirable behaviors. The degree of sophistication they use varies according to their age and developmental level, as well as the complexity of skills to be learned.

Self-management can be defined as the engineering of an individual's social and physical environment to increase the likelihood of reinforcers being provided for behaviors that are positive in their effect in the long term and/or reduce the likelihood of reinforcing behaviors that are negative in their effect in the long term. The emphasis is upon antecedent control prior to the behavior to increase or decrease the likelihood of a given set of responses and arranging for other individuals or oneself to provide consequences for certain responses.

A Synopsis of the Self-Management Process

The initial step in the self-management process is to identify a problem. A student can often assist with this task. Then the behavior is operationalized, or stated in observable terms. The next step is to select an accurate and reliable measurement system. The student then applies the system and records behavior counts. "Bugs" are worked out, and results are displayed graphically. If results are stable, the student and/or advisor select(s) a technique of behavior change involving antecedents and/or consequences. The systematic use of antecedents and consequences is what makes self-management more sophisticated than self-monitoring *per se*. A behavior change design, probably a changing criterion, is then selected. The student continues to plot behavioral counts to determine whether they indicate a steady change in the desired direction. If desired results are not attained within a reasonable time (i.e., a week or so), the system is reevaluated. Necessary changes are made, and the process begins anew.

When reinforcement is part of a behavior change program, a changing criterion design is often used. This design provides gradual step improvements in the targeted behavior before reinforcement occurs (*see* Figures 9-1 and 9-2). Gradual increases or decreases over prior baseline levels of the targeted behavior can more realistically be achieved than immediately changing from baseline to desired levels. For example, it is easier to stop smoking by making gradual reductions than it is to stop "cold turkey."

Reviewing the *ABC*s of Behavior Change

This section reviews the *ABC*s of behavior change in terms of their role in self-management. The three components were initially described in Chapter 1.

Behavior

The focus of the preceding eight chapters has been on self-monitoring. Our discussions have included such techniques as recording one's own behavior each time it occurs (i.e., event recording), marking whether a behavior is occurring when an audio cue is heard at regular or random intervals (i.e., time sampling), and placing a mark on notecards or charts when students "think of it." Students were also taught to score their behavior according to certain criteria (i.e., self-evaluation). These skills involve the student in the *B* part of the *ABC*s of behavior change. That is, the student to some degree is taking control of

THE RADICAL BEHAVIORIST APPROACH TO BEHAVIORAL SELF-MANAGEMENT

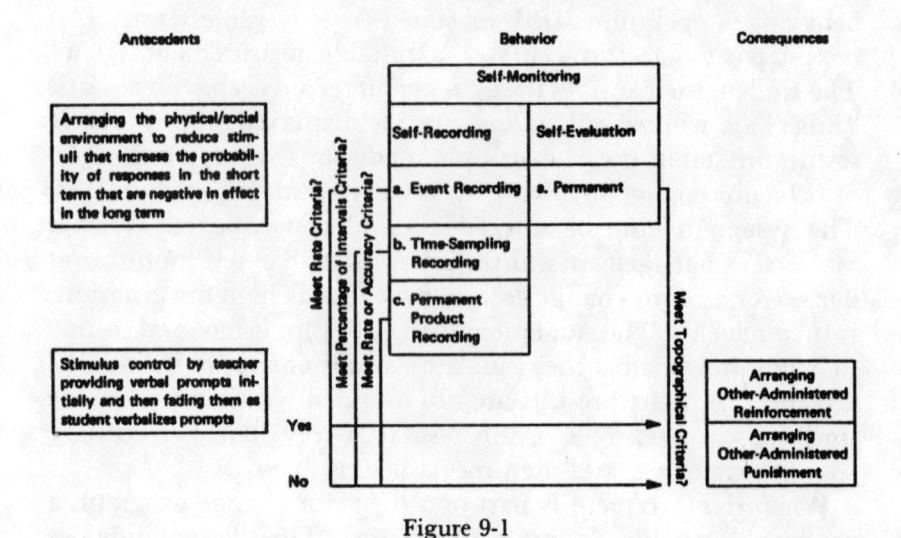

Figure 9-1

Instructions: Place a tally mark each time you interrupt the teacher during his or her lecture with comments unrelated to the topic being discussed.

Period/Class
============

English   ///
Math   /////
Social Studies //

Figure 9-2. Self-tallying example.

recording his or her *behavior*. This text is designed primarily to deal with self-monitoring and includes only basic reviews of the general principles underlying behavior change. For a more detailed review of the general principles of behavior change, the reader is referred to Alberto and Troutman (1982) or Sulzer-Azaroff and Mayer (1977).

Consequences

We have discussed several studies of solving practical problems in the classroom through self-monitoring. Many of these studies have involved the use of teacher-controlled or student-controlled *consequences* (i.e., the *C* of the *ABC*s). As we stated in Chapter 1, consequences are events that immediately follow a behavior. Their result may be to increase the future occurrence of a behavior (i.e., reinforcing), decrease the future occurrence of the behavior (i.e., punishing), or have little or no effect upon the behavior (i.e., neutral). The only test of the effects of a specific consequence with a given individual is to record the impact of the consequence upon the behavior it normally follows. Few consequences have an immediate effect on behavior. Most take several days to a week to produce appreciable change.

When a student controls in some way the consequences of his or her behavior, this is behavioral self-management. In many cases a teacher totally controls the consequences of student behavior. This is not behavioral self-management. In other cases the teacher initially controls the consequences, while the student gradually assumes increasing amounts of control. This represents a shift from teacher- to self-management. In studies in which the student controls the consequences of his or her behavior, bonuses have often been provided for students who match teacher records or ratings of behavior. Penalties for failing to match teacher records or ratings have also been used. Checks between teacher and student records or ratings are generally reduced to a minimum over time.

Antecedents

Antecedents, the *A* of the *ABC*s of behavior change, are those stimuli and events that precede a behavior. When these stimuli or events regularly precede a behavior and increase or decrease the likelihood of its occurring, they are said to be exerting antecedent, or stimulus, *control*. Antecedent control, however, is closely linked to the consequences of behavior. In fact, antecedent control is dependent upon past consequences of the specific behaviors.

For example, a library has many stimuli that exert antecedent stimuli over behavior. Stacks of books, signs, study carrels, peacefulness, and the librarian's presence tend to reduce visitor speech in terms of volume and frequency. This is due to the previous punishing consequences the individual has received for speaking loudly or frequently in libraries. It is certainly not due to the books, carrels, or librarian *per se*.

A teacher who says, "All children finishing their work can go to recess early" may find several children hastily writing answers. Other children may appear unaffected by the announcement. Students who rush to complete their work probably find recess reinforcing, have had other teachers or the same one make similar statements that led to reinforcers, are able to do the work fluently, and/or are unconcerned about accuracy. Students who continued as before may find other activities more reinforcing than recess, not have experienced adults or teachers making similar statements that led to reinforcers, and/or receive reinforcers for accurate work that are more powerful than those from extra recess.

In the studies we cited in Chapters 5 through 8, antecedent control was generally better developed in mature individuals than it was in children. Also, most cases involved antecedent control exerted by other individuals rather than by those persons engaged in self-monitoring. As individuals move from exclusive use of self-monitoring to include self-management, they also learn the value of antecedent control.

Integrating the ABCs

Brigham (1982) cited a case study involving an adolescent female arranging for a relative to administer punishers to reduce weight. She collected baseline data on her eating habits and daily weight. She operationalized good and poor eating habits and selected as an intervention technique a response cost procedure in which she gave her sister fifty cents for an established frequency of poor eating habits. This led to a decrease in poor eating habits and subsequent weight loss.

One important element in this form of consequence is the involvement of another, preferably trusted, individual to administer the consequences. A verbal or written contract may be used to establish the contingency. The contingency may involve reinforcers as well as punishers that are administered by others. A second critical component is prior training in simple applied behavior analysis in order to design an intervention program. The training of students in simple principles of behavior management can also be used when the student must modify the social environment (e.g., what friends say) by altering his or her behavior (e.g., ignoring certain verbalizations). In this way a student can reduce the frequency of verbal punishers and increase the verbal reinforcers received from other individuals.

Planned reinforcement by students to alter the reinforcers and punishers received from others can be used when a student is trying to overcome a bad reputation. The student may have previously earned the reputation. However, he or she has changed the problem behaviors. This situation was encountered by Graubard, Rosenberg, and Miller (1971). The previously problem students had changed their behavior but continued to receive reprimands from teachers and peers based upon previous behavior,

The students were taught the techniques of ignoring these reprimands and politely thanking the teachers for providing additional assistance, complimenting their appearance, and commenting on their improved behavior. The teachers were so unaccustomed to these reinforcers that their verbal behavior was dramatically altered.

The same techniques can be used to change peers' verbal behavior. Solomon and Wahler (1973) reported that social attention by peers for "disruptive" students was focused on the deviant behavior almost exclusively and served to reinforce it. In this way students who develop a bad reputation can alter their social environment to provide reinforcers for appropriate behavior and avoid the almost inevitable cycle of going from a poor reputation to juvenile delinquency to dropping out of school, unemployment, petty crimes, or prostitution.

Two Types of Self-Management: Cognitive Behaviorism and Radical Behaviorism

Two groups of researchers have traditionally assumed responsibility for behavioral self-management. These groups have been labeled *cognitive behavior modifiers* (CBM)(Meichenbaum, 1977) and *radical behaviorists* (RB)(Brigham, 1982a). Radical behaviorists have continued the tradition of B.F. Skinner (1953) by focusing on behavior that is directly observable by several independent observers. Cognitive behaviorists have introduced the study of an individual's private or covert thoughts, beliefs, and attitudes as target behaviors, consequences, and antecedents in the self-management process. Both groups acknowledge that these responses occur. However, the RB advocates contend that their function is not controlling behavior, but merely is descriptive of relationships between responses and the actual variables that control environment (Jaynes, 1977).

Self-management research has become a natural focal point for the dispute between these two groups of behaviorists due to the implied cognitive aspects of "self"-control. The groups have differed primarily in terms of the importance and function of self-administered consequences and antecedents. To CBM researchers, self-reinforcement is an established procedure for increasing behavior. To RB researchers, there are serious questions about whether self-reinforcement follows the same principles and has the same effect as other-administered reinforcers. The basic procedures, however, appear on the surface to be similar (Brigham, 1982a).

If an individual has free access to a reinforcer and postpones its administration until he or she meets some criterion of a task, this process is far different from the common examples of reinforcement administered by others and may have very different effects. Also, it would be surprising if an individual did not stop a task at any moment and self-administer the reinforcer prior to task completion. If an individual does indeed postpone the accessible reinforcer until task criteria are met, this is a form of self-management and probably due to aversive consequences for early administration of the reinforcer (Skinner, 1953). The source for these aversive consequences can probably be found in the individual's history of contact with reinforcers and punishers in the social environment.

To the RB manager, the focus of acquiring self-control is the arranging of the environment to reduce the likelihood of encountering other-administered reinforcers that are viewed favorably in the short term but may have long-term aversive consequences. This process is similar to the concern of parents about their children selecting friends carefully. Students who select friends who provide reinforcers for studying, practicing sports or musical instruments, eating properly, or exercising increase the likelihood that they will acquire important skills and healthy habits. Examples of poor arranging of the environment include selecting friends who smoke, play video games instead of studying, engage in shoplifting, speed in an automobile, eat large amounts of sweets, and abuse drugs, along with innumerable other common problems of self-management in today's children and youth.

The physical environment can also be arranged similarly by removing sources of reinforcement for short-term behaviors that are aversive in the long term. Cigarettes, sweets, video games, drugs, and alcohol can be removed from the living area, while textbooks, healthy foods, and exercise equipment are made easily accessible. Individuals who arrange their environment to encounter long-term rather than short-term reinforcers are said to possess self-control. Individuals who encounter short-term reinforcers at the expense of long-term consequences are said to need self-management skills.

Self-instruction is another point of disagreement among CBM and RB researchers. The self-instructional steps previously cited from Meichenbaum and Goodman (1971) include covert events that are not subject to study by RB researchers. To RB researchers, the covert events are ignored, and the process described is one of the teacher providing prompts until the student can perform the overt behavior of interest (e.g., completing written assignments without error).

A point raised by Brigham (1982a) is that CBM researchers often achieve behavior change via potent but misunderstood and mislabeled independent variables. For example, the self-instructional program of Meichenbaum and Goodman (1971) employs teacher instructions that are gradually faded. This is a form of the well-established behavioral principle of stimulus control. It is useful for acquiring new behaviors if the covert steps are ignored. Brigham's position is that many of the positive changes in behavior achieved by CBM researchers employ independent variables that also may be potentially mislabeled.

General Suggestions for Teaching Self-Management

Marshall and Heward (1979) described what may be an ideal way to teach self-management, called the Visual Response System (VRS). They used a specially designed classroom in which eight to ten students wrote responses on an overhead project built into each desk. Their responses were projected on a wall behind them. Two advantages of the VRS: (1) The opportunity for student response is maximized. Every student responds to every question or problem as opposed to responding only when called upon in a typical group. (2) Visual access to student responses as they are emitted enables a teacher to deliver reinforcement and/or remediation in a direct, continuous, and virtually immediate fashion (p. 216).

An additional advantage of the VRS involves the use on a regular basis of projectors to display the results of each individual's self-management project in its various stages. In this manner, students can profit from their peers' self-management projects and thus be better prepared to manage a wide variety of behaviors. A thermal copier capable of making overhead transparencies would be a nice addition to the classroom. This would allow recording forms, sample graphs, designs, and other information to be displayed easily.

Unfortunately, most teachers do not have the option of using a visual response system and have at best one overhead projector or perhaps a chalkboard for display purposes. Self-management, like most skills, can be effectively taught with much simpler apparatus. In fact, the individuals involved are far more critical than any apparatus.

A highly successful method for teaching self-management to students includes pairing procedural lessons with individual behavior change programs. Several suggested lessons are included below. Lessons should be presented as they occur naturally in the behavior management project. An excellent resource for additional information on self-management is provided in *Managing Everyday Problems: A Manual of Applied Psychology for Young People* (Brigham, 1982b).

Lesson 1—Identifying a Target Behavior and Deciding When to Count

Objectives:
1. The student, when given a list of characteristics, will write the specific observable behaviors that can be counted or evaluated.
2. The student, when given a list of behaviors that can and cannot be objectively counted or evaluated, will mark the ones written in an objective manner.

Activities:

Students can listen or read about differences between characteristics and identify one or more observable behaviors per characteristic. This can be done individually or in small groups. Each student or group should be given the same list of characteristics. The result should be different observable behaviors for each person or group if they do not consult each other. This exercise should emphasize the need for less ambiguous terms.

One of the most serious problems in society today is the inability to communicate accurately and reliably. In watching local television news and comparing it to national news broadcasts, we typically find that the national broadcasters speak more precisely. They also appear to be more careful of what they say.

The reason that news broadcasters must be careful with their speech is that the English language tends to be confusing. They find it much simpler to report exactly what they or their colleagues see. They rarely say that the president has done something "wrong" or an athlete has said something "stupid." Rather, they report what the president did or an athlete said as precisely as possible. The viewer is then free to make value judgments about the behaviors.

Scientists who study physics, biology, chemistry, medicine, or psychology must be even more careful with their statements. When we observe a respected scientist reporting his or her research, we see the importance scientists place on limiting sensationalism and subjectivity.

One of the skills necessary to record behavior is the use of words that specify what has been seen, no more and no less. A dictionary typically includes several meanings for most words, and some may have as many as eight, ten, or more definitions.

For our purposes there are two types of words. The first are words (and phrases) that describe general characteristics, such as *mean, weak, smart, popular, a loner, a troublemaker, a good dresser,* etc. These words have many different meanings. The other type, used by behavioral specialists, is *specific terms*, like *hitting, doing push-ups, answering a teacher's questions,* and *talking to friends.* The advantage of this second type of words is that we can actually count and record the number of times that the behaviors they name occur.

Lesson 2—Recording Techniques

Objectives:
1. The student will observe one form of his or her behavior and record it using a simple tallying procedure.
2. The student will observe one form of his or her behavior and record it using a time-sampling procedure.
3. The student will observe one form of his or her behavior and rate it using a self-evaluation procedure.

Activities:

The teacher should help each student select a specific behavior that both consider in need of improvement. The teacher and student should observe during the same time periods and compare results. Tallying should be used with behaviors that are easy to count (i.e., hits, push-ups). It is also necessary for both persons to have sufficient time to make tallies after each behavior.

Time sampling should be used with behaviors that are not easy to count. These behaviors include temper tantrums, walking around the room, and staring off into space. Time sampling is also used when either the teacher or the student cannot be interrupted from work on an irregular basis.

Self-evaluation should be used with these behaviors for which a qualitative measure is more appropriate than a quantitative one. Examples of such behaviors include handwriting, dancing, and gymnastics.

Permanent product recording should be used with behaviors that leave written evidence that an event has occurred: Examples include math problems completed correctly on a worksheet and written answers to reading comprehension questions. This recording procedure is also useful with other types of observable evidence (e.g., shirts folded properly, beds made, bicycle parts assembled properly).

Self-tallying can be used with behaviors that do not leave observable proof. This procedure should also be used when the counting procedure does not interrupt the behavior appreciably, as it would if a student tried to tally oral reading errors. It can also be used with inappropriate classroom behaviors, such as interrupting the teacher (Figure 9-2).

Figures and applications for time sampling can be found in Figure 5-1 and Figure 8-1. Figures 6-1 and 6-2 are samples of self-evaluation. Permanent product recording examples can be found in Chapter 5, including Figures 5-2 and 5-3.

Lesson 3—Arranging Consequences

Objectives:
1. The student will accurately define in simple terms *reinforcement* and *response cost*.
2. The student will list potential reinforcers and punishers that have personal meaning.
3. The student will write proper behavioral contracts, with reinforcers and/or response cost consequences.

Activities:

The students should read or be taught in lecture format the section in Chapter 2 entitled "The Consequences of Behavior." Students should focus on the concept of reinforcement and response cost as alternatives in self-arranging consequences. The general approach is to arrange for a trusted adult or peer to assist the student in administering consequences. One potential reinforcer is money (e.g., earning from ten cents to a dollar each day or week in which the behavior improves). Another option is to use a short-term activity reinforcer (e.g., access to watching a favorite television show). A long-term activity reinforcer (e.g., attending a football game with a parent or teacher) in which points are earned over several weeks is a third choice. These options may be used in various combinations as well.

Response cost can be explained by comparing it to traffic fines. The term means that certain types and levels of response cause persons to lose money or privileges. They "cost" the person. For example, a type of response that often costs a person is driving through a red light or stop sign. A level of response would be driving above the speed limit. Student's levels of response may cost them money and privileges. With both the driver and the student, the goal is to change the individual's behavior, as well as to help others (e.g., to reduce traffic accidents involving others or help the teacher do his or her job effectively).

If response cost is involved, a student may lose money for failing to meet an appropriate goal. The same approach can be used with the loss of short-term activity reinforcers or points toward a long-term activity reinforcer. Two critical aspects of response cost are to make the required criteria fair (i.e., readily achievable) and to arrange requirements so that students do not "go in the hole," or lose all reinforcers.

The manner in which criteria for improvement are determined is to collect baseline data for several days before beginning the program. Even gradual improvements should earn reinforcers or avoid response cost. Students who are making disruptive comments at an average baseline level of ten per period should be expected to reduce these by approximately two per week (e.g., to eight, six, four, two) until an acceptable level is obtained. A criterion of zero responses should never be used. A student who is correctly completing 50 percent of his or her math problems during baseline should have as a weekly criterion a 5 (e.g., to 55, 60, 65 percent) or 10 percent increase (e.g., to 60, 70, 80, 90 percent). In the case of a behavior that a student is trying in increase, a 100 percent criterion should be avoided, and 95 percent used.

The first step in the student project is for baseline data to be collected for at least three days. Then a reasonable criterion for improvement can be determined. Next, the student, with the teacher's assistance, forms a written contact between himself or herself and the trusted adult or peer. The contract should be written or revised on a weekly basis and specify the behavior required, the consequences (i.e., reinforcer and/or response cost), and the criteria to earn reinforcers or avoid response cost. Then the student and the adult or peer signs it. If response cost is to be used, it is critical that the peer or adult entering the contract have control over the reinforcers. The student, for example, may deposit and receive a receipt for five dollars with the adult or peer. The contract could look something like the one in Figure 9-3.

Students vary in their ability to select reinforcers. Some may need a list. Others may need to consult friends or parents about what they enjoy. If a student consistently fails to meet the criterion for reinforcement or avoid response cost, a change to be made in either the criterion or the reinforcer.

Lesson 4–Arranging Antecedents or Stimulus Control
Objectives:
   1. The student, when given a list of problem behaviors, will

Self-Management: The Completed Process

I, _____ (student's name) _____

will _____ (student's behavior) _____ during the

week of _____ (date) _____ at a level of

_____ (criteria for improvement) _____ in order to

receive _____ (quantity and type of reinforcers) _____

or lose _____ (quantity and type of response cost) _____

Signed _____ (student's signature) _____

Signed _____ (other adult or peer's signature) _____

Figure 9-3. Sample contract

identify reasonable ways to arrange antecedents to increase or decrease each item.
2. The student will state in simple terms how antecedent control works.

Activities:

The teacher should review in Chapter 2 the section on antecedents. The main points are that antecedent control is present and exerted before a behavior occurs and the result of consequences students have encountered for past behaviors. Several sections in the chapters on academics, inappropriate classroom behaviors, and vocational/self-help skills include the use of antecedent control. Antecedent control includes visual and auditory prompts, as well as models. The example in Chapter 2 under "Antecedents" is a sequence of auditory cues that were initially modeled by the teacher and then said by the student. Chapter 5 described a poster of rules for staying on task. Also, self-monitoring notecards and charts have been used as antecedents, as they were in controlling off-task behaviors (*see* Figure 5-1). In addition, Chapter 5 included a study in which students learned to isolate themselves for periods of time to study. This, too, is a form of antecedent control. It is sometimes called *stimulus control*. In this case the student is removing himself or herself from stimuli that compete with studying.

The section on handwriting in Chapter 5 may be helpful in learning antecedent control. The self-evaluation techniques described in this section also exert control over handwriting by alerting the student to the required criteria (i.e., slant, spacing, formation).

The most elaborate form of antecedent control was described in the section on written expression in Chapter 5. Auditory cues were provided by the operational definitions of sentences, action words, describing words, and on-task behavior. The wall charts were probably the most effective example (i.e., descriptions of sentences, how to select a topic, proper writing behavior, sample topical nouns for writing themes).

In Chapter 6, the self-monitoring notecard in Figure 6-1 or 6-2 could produce antecedent control. A chart of classroom rules could also exert similar control, as might the "turtle technique." The prior consequences of behavior in the presence of a particular antecedent normally determine whether inappropriate behavior will be reduced.

Students can include these forms of antecedent control as part of their self-management program. For example, they can use their own auditory cues to aid in task completion. They can post rules or operational definitions for desirable or undesirable behaviors. They can isolate themselves to reduce competing stimuli while studying. They can observe models of a behavior they want to improve, such as a skilled peer demonstrating penmanship or a famous quarterback throwing a pass. They can also provide themselves with posters, pictures, books, or other stimuli that increase the likelihood of desired behavior.

Lesson 5—Learning Design and Graphic Display

Objectives:

1. The student will, when given data, chart the information on a simple graph.
2. The student will, when given a behavior and criteria for

Self-Management: The Completed Process

consequences, label the axes and draw an appropriate changing criterion design.

Activities:

A simple graphic display of data is quite easy to do once Lessons 1 through 4 have been completed. A suggested way to graph data is to label the horizontal axis in terms of consecutive school days (for behaviors that occur only in school) or merely consecutive days (if the behavior occurs on weekends as well).

The vertical axis is labeled by the type of behavior in the project (e.g., talk-outs in class, minutes on task, assignments completed, pounds lost). It is divided by the units of measurement (e.g., percentage correct). The axis is divided into units from zero to the ceiling (e.g., 100 percent). With other units, the artificial "ceiling" should be slightly above the greatest number of units expected (e.g., twenty talk-outs per period, fifty minutes on task per period, five pounds lost per day). The vertical axis should began at zero and be divided into units up to the arbitrary ceiling.

The changing criterion design closely relates to the suggested contracting procedure in Lesson 4. The weeks are separated by vertical lines, and the criteria for improvement taken directly from the contract. The criteria are then plotted as a horizontal line (Figures 9-4 and 9-5). Data points should be lined up with the appropriate day from the horizontal axis and appropriate unit from the vertical axis.

Baseline data are charted along with the behaviors that follow. If the data stay close to the criterion lines and increase or decrease at roughly the same time the criteria change, this simple design provides evidence that self-monitoring is working. It also il-

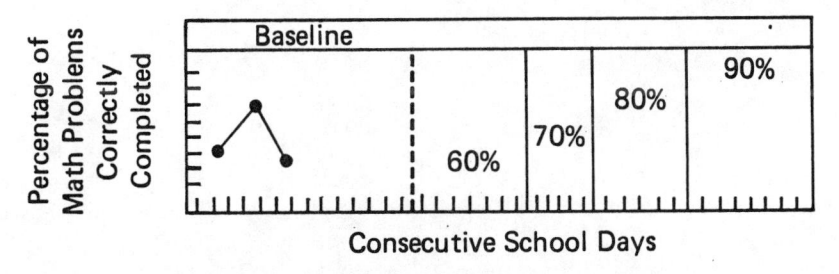

Figure 9-4. A graph with a natural ceiling using a changing criterion design.

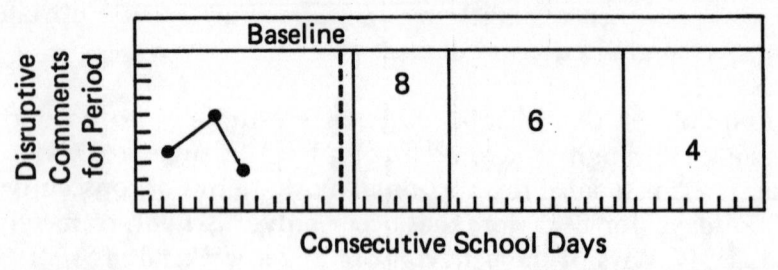

Figure 9-5. A graph with an arbitrary ceiling using a changing criterion design.

lustrates how effective it is. Criteria may be increased or decreased according to how easily they are attained.

Conclusion

Hopefully, as students complete their self-management projects and observe other students' implementing theirs, they will gradually acquire the skills necessary to manage problem behavior effectively. A basic understanding of the options they have should facilitate the process. These options include observing, arranging consequences and antecedents, setting satisfactory criteria for success, and graphing and evaluating data. With practice and patience, students will discover the pleasures of being able to exert personal control over their daily behavior.

References

Alberto, P. A., & Troutman, A. C. *Applied behavior analysis for teachers: Influencing student performance.* Columbus: Charles E. Merrill, 1982.

Alden, L., Safran, J., & Weideman, R. A comparison of cognitive and skills training strategies in the treatment of unassertive clients. *Behavior Therapy,* 1979, 9, 843, 846.

Anton, J. L., Dunbar, J., & Friedman, L. Anticipation training in the treatment of depression. In J. D. Krumboltz & C. E. Thoreson (Eds.), *Counseling methods.* New York: Holt, Rinehart, & Winston, 1976.

Azrin, N., & Powell, J. Behavioral engineering: The reduction of smoking behavior by a conditioned apparatus and procedure. *Journal Of Applied Behavior Analysis,* 1968, 1, 193-200.

Azrin, N., Rubin, H., O'Brien, F., Ayllon, T., & Roll, D. Behavioral engineering: Postural control by a portable operant apparatus. *Journal of Applied Behavior Analysis,* 1968, 1, 99-108.

Bailey, C. D. Students' self-assessment: Helping students help themselves. *Kappa Delta Pi Record,* 1979, 15, 86-88, 96.

Ballard, K.D., & Glynn, T. Behavioral self-management in story writing with elementary school children. *Journal of Applied Behavior Analysis,* 1975, 8, 387-398.

Barkley, R. A., Copeland, A. P., & Sivage, C. A self-control classroom for hyperactive children. *Journal of Autism and Developmental Disabilities,* 1980, 10, 75-89.

Barrios, B., & Shigetomi, C. Coping skills training: Potential for prevention of fears and anxieties. *Behavior Therapy,* 1980, 11, 431-439.

Bates, S., & Bates, D. F. . . .And a child shall teach them. *Teaching Exceptional Children,* 1971, 3, 111-113.

Bernstein, D. A., & Borkovec, T. D. *Progressive relaxation training: A manual for the helping professions.* Champaign, IL: Research Press, 1973.

Bornstein, P. H., & Quevillon, R. P. The effect of a self-instructional package on overactive preschool boys. *Journal of Applied Behavior Analysis,* 1976, 9, 179-188.

Brigham, T. Self-management: A radical behavioral perspective. In P. Karoly & F. H. Kanfer (Eds.), *Self-management and behavior change.* New York: Pergamon Press, 1982. (a)

Brigham, T.A. Managing everyday problems: A manual of applied psychology for young people. Unpublished manuscript, Washington State University, 1982. (b)

Broden, M., Hall, R. V., & Mitts, B. The effect of self-recording on the classroom behavior of two eighth-grade students. *Journal of Applied Behavior Analysis,* 1971, *4,* 191-199.

Cartwright, C.A., & Cartwright, G.P. *Developing observation skills.* New York: McGraw-Hill, 1974.

Ciminero, A.R., Nelson, R.O., & Lipinski, D.P. Self-monitoring procedures. In A.R. Ciminero, K.S. Calhoun, & H.E. Adams (Eds.), *Handbook of behavioral assessment.* New York: John Wiley and Sons, 1977.

Congressional Record, October 10, 1978, H-12179.

Cooley, E.J., & Spiegler, M.D. Cognitive versus emotional coping responses as alternatives to test anxiety. *Cognitive Therapy and Research,* 1980, *4,* 159-166.

Csapo, M. The effect of self recording and social reinforcement components of parent training programs. *Journal of Experimental Child Psychology,* 1979, *27,* 384-394.

Davis, J.K., & Rand, D.C. Self-grading versus instructor grading. *Journal of Educational Research,* 1980, *73,* 207-211.

Dickerson, E.A., & Creedon, C.F. Self-selection of standards by children: The relative effectiveness of pupil-selected and teacher-selected standards of performance. *Journal of Applied Behavior Analysis,* 1981, *14,* 425-433.

Federal Register. Education of all handicapped children act, August 23, 1977, 42478.

Fremouw, W.J., & Zitter, R.E. A comparison of skills training and cognitive restructuring relaxation for the treatment of speech anxiety. *Behavior Therapy,* 1978, *9,* 248-259.

Friedling, C., & O'Leary, S.G. Effects of self-instructional training on second and third grade hyperactive children: A failure to replicate. *Journal of Applied Behavior Analysis,* 1979, *12,* 211-219.

Glynn, E.L., Thomas, J.D., & Shee, S.M. Behavioral self-control of on-task behavior in an elementary classroom. *Journal of Applied Behavior Analysis,* 1973, *6,* 105-113.

Goldiamond, I. Self-control procedures in personal behavior problems. *Psychological Reports,* 1965, *17,* 851-868.

Graubard, P.S., Rosenberg, H., & Miller, M.B. Student applications of behavior modification to teachers and environments or ecological approaches to social deviancy. In E.A. Ramp & B. L. Hopkins (Eds.), *A new direction for education: Behavior analysis.* University of Kansas, 1971.

Grossman, H.J. (Ed). *Manual on terminology and classification in mental retardation.* Washington, D.C.: American Association on Mental Deficiency, 1973.

References

Hannum, J. W., Thoreson, C. E., & Hubbard, D. R. A behavioral study of self-esteem with elementary teachers. In M. J. Mahoney & C. E. Thoreson (Eds.), *Self-control: Power to the person.* Monterey, CA: Brooks-Cole, 1974.

Hansen, C. L. Writing skills. In N. G. Haring, T. C. Lovitt, M. D. Eaton, & C. L. Hansen (Eds.), *The fourth R: Research in the classroom.* Columbus, OH: Charles E. Merrill, 1978.

Haring, N. G., Eaton, M. D., Lovitt, T. C., & Hansen, C. L. (Eds.). *The fourth R: Research in the classroom.* Columbus, OH: Charles E. Merrill, 1978.

Harris, G., & Johnson, S. B. Comparison of individualized overt modeling, desensitization, and study skills training for alleviation of test anxiety. *Journal of Counseling and Clinical Psychology,* 1980, *48,* 1986-194.

Hefferman, T., & Richards, C.S. Self-control of study behavior: Identification and evaluation of natural methods. *Journal of Counseling Psychology,* 1981, *28,* 361-364.

Helwig, J. J., Jones, J.C., Norman, J. E., & Cooper, J. O. The measurement of manuscript letter strokes. *Journal of Applied Behavior Analysis,* 1976, *9,* 231-236.

Heward, W. L., & Orlansky, M.D. *Exceptional children.* Columbus, OH: Charles E. Merrill, 1980.

Homme, L. E. Perspectives in psychology, XXIV: Control of coverance, the operant of the mind. *Psychological Record,* 1965, *15,* 501-511.

Horner, R. H., & Brigham, T. A. The effects of self-management procedures on the study behavior of two retarded children. *Education and Training of the Mentally Retarded,* 1979, *14,* 18-24.

Hundert, T., & Bucher, B. Pupils' self-scored arithmetic performance: A practical procedure for maintaining accurancy. *Journal of Applied Behavior Analysis,* 1978, *11,* 304.

Jackson, H. J., & Boag, P. G. The efficacy of self control procedures as motivational strategies with mentally retarded persons: A review of the literature and guidelines for future research. *Australian Journal of Developmental Disabilities,* 1981, 7, 65-79.

Jacobsen, E. *Progressive relaxation.* Chicago: University of Chicago Press, 1983.

Jaynes, J. *The origins of consciousness in the breakdown of the bicameral mind.* Boston: Houghton Mifflin, 1977.

Johnson, W. G. Some applications of Homme's coverant control therapy: Two case reports. *Behavior Therapy,* 1971, 21,240-248.

Jones, J. C., Trap, J. & Cooper, J. O. Technical report: Students' self-recording of manuscript letter strokes. *Journal of Applied Behavior Analysis,* 1977, *10,* 509-514.

Kanter, N. J., & Goldfried, M.R. Relative effectiveness of relational restructuring self-control desensitization in the reduction of interpersonal anxiety. *Behavior Therapy,* 1979, *10,* 472-490.

Karoly, P., & Kanfer, F. H. *Self-management and behavior change: From theory to practice.* New York: Pergamon International Library, 1982.

Kauffman, J. M. *Characteristics of children's behavioral disorders* (2nd ed.). Columbus, OH: Charles E. Merrill, 1981.

Kazdin, A. E. Reactive self-monitoring: The effects of response durability, goal setting and feedback. *Journal of Consulting and Clinical Psychology*, 1974, *42*, 704-716. (a)

Kazdin, A. E. Self-monitoring and behavior change. In M. J. Mahoney & C. E. Thoreson (Eds.), *Self-control: Power to the person.* Monterey, CA: Brooks-Cole, 1974. (b)

Kunzelman, H. D. (Ed.). *Precision teaching.* Seattle: Special Child Publications, 1970.

Lewinsohn, P. M., Biglan, A., & Zeiss, A. M. Behavioral treatment of depression. In P. O. Davidson (Ed.), *The behavioral management of anxiety, depression, and pain.* New York: Brunner/Mazel, 1976.

Lewinsohn, P. M., Mischel, W., Chaplin, W., & Barton, R. Social competence and depression: The role of illusory self-perceptions. *Journal of Abnormal Psychology*, 1980, *89*, 203-213.

Lewinsohn, P. M., & Talkington, J. Studies on the measurement of unpleasant events and relations with depression. *Applied Psychological Measurement*, 1979, *3*, 83-101.

Lobitz, W. C., & Lopiccolo, J. New methods in the behavioral treatment of sexual dysfunction. *Journal of Behavior Therapy and Experimental Psychiatry*, 1972, *3*, 265-271.

Lowe, J. C. & Mikulas, W. L. Use of written material in learning self-control of premature ejaculation. *Psychological Reports*, 1975, *37*, 295-298.

Madsen, C. H., & Ullman, L. P. Innovations in the desensitization of frigidity. *Behavior Research and Therapy*, 1967, *5*, 67-68.

Mahoney, M. J. The self-management of covert behavior: A case study. *Behavior Therapy*, 1971, *2*, 575-78.

Mahoney, M. J. Self-reward and self-monitoring techniques for weight control. *Behavior Therapy*, 1974, *5*, 48-57.

Mahoney, M. J., & Thoreson, C. E. (Eds.). *Self-control: Power to the person.* Monterey, CA: Brooks-Cole, 1974.

Mahoney, M. J., Thoreson, C. E., & Danaher, B. G. Covert Behavior modification: An experimental analogue. *Journal of Behavior Therapy and Experimental Psychiatry*, 1972, *3*, 7-14.

Marshall, A. E., & Heward, W. L. Teaching self-management to incarcerated youth. *Behavioral Disorders*, 1979, *4*, 215-226.

Matson, J. L., Marchetti, A., & Adkins, J. Comparison of operant and independence-trained procedures for mentally retarded adults. *American Journal of Mental Deficiency*, 1980, *84*, 487-494.

McLaughlin, T. F. Self-control in the classroom. *Review of Educational Research*, 1976, *46*, 631-663.

McMullen, S., & Rosen, R. C. Self-administered masturbation training in the treatment of primary orgasmic dysfunction. *Journal of Consulting and Clinical Psychology*, 1979, *47*, 912-918.

Meichenbaum, D. H. *Cognitive behavior modification: An integrative approach.* New York: Plenum Press, 1977.

Meichenbaum, D. H., & Goodman, J. Training impulsive children to talk to themselves: A means of developing self-control. *Journal of Abnormal Psychology,* 1971, 77, 115-126.

Meyer, H. H. Self appraisal of job performance. *Personnel Psychology,* 1980, 33, 291-95.

Nathan, M., Millham, J., Chilcutt, J., & Atkinson, B. Mentally retarded individuals as informants for the AAMD Adaptive Behavior Scale. *Mental Retardation,* 1980, 18, 82-84.

O'Leary, S. G., & Dubey, D. R. Application of self-control procedures by children: A review. *Journal of Applied Behavior Analysis,* 1979, 12, 449-465.

Peacock, R., Layman, R. D., & Richard, H. C. Correspondence between self-report and observer as a function of task difficulty. *Behavior Therapy,* 1978, 9, 578-583.

Piersall, W. C., & Kratochwill, T. R. Self-observation and behavior change: Applications to academic and adjustment problems through behavioral consultation. *Journal of School Psychology,* 1979, 17, 151-161

Polsgrove, L. Self-control: Methods for child training. *Behavioral Disorders,* 1979, 4, 116-130.

Robin, A., Schneider, M., & Dolnick, M. The turtle technique: An extended case study of self-control in the classroom. In I. D. O'Leary & S. G. O'Leary (Eds.), *Classroom management: The successful use of behavior modification.* New York: Pergamon Press, 1977.

Rosenbaum, M. S., & Drabman, R. S. Self-control training in the classroom: A review and critique. *Journal of Applied Behavior Analysis,* 1979, 12, 467-485.

Ruppel, G. Self-management and reading rate improvement. *Journal of Counseling Psychology,* 1979, 26, 451-454.

Rush, A. J., Beck, A. T., Kovacs, M., & Hollon, S. Comparative efficacy of cognitive therapy and pharmacotherapy in the treatment of depressed outpatients. *Cognitive Therapy and Research,* 1977, 1, 17-38.

Sagotsky, G., Patterson, C. J., & Lepper, M. R. Training children's self-control: A field experiment in self-monitoring and goal setting in the classroom. *Journal of Experimental Child Psychology,* 1978, 25, 242-253.

Schulmann, J. L., & Reisman, J. M. An objective measurement of hyperactivity. *American Journal of Mental Deficiency,* 1959, 64, 455-456.

Seymour, F. W., & Stokes, T. F. Self-recording in training girls to increase work and evoke staff praise in an institution for offenders. *Journal of Applied Behavior Analysis,* 1976, 9, 41-54.

Sheehan, D. J., & Casey, B. Communication. *Journal of Applied Behavior Analysis,* 1974, 7, 446.

Skinner, B. F. *Science and human behavior.* New York: Macmillan Publishing Company, 1953.

Skinner, B. F. *Verbal behavior.* Englewood Cliffs, NJ: Prentice-Hall, 1957.

Solomon, R. W., & Wahler, R. G. Peer reinforcement control of classroom problem behavior. *Journal of Applied Behavior Analysis,* 1973, *6,* 49-56.

Stokes, T. F., & Baer, D. M. An implicit technology of generalization. *Journal of Applied Behavior Analysis,* 1977, *10,* 349-367.

Sulzer-Azaroff, B., & Mayer, C. R. *Applying behavior-analysis procedures with children and youth.* New York: Holt, Rinehart, and Winston, 1977.

Swanson, L. Modification of comprehension deficits in learning disabled children. *Learning Disabilities Quarterly,* 1981, *4,* 189-202.

Tharp, R., Watson, D. L., & Daya, J. Self-modification of depression. *Journal of Consulting and Clinical Psychology,* 1974, *42,* 624.

Tharp, R., & Wetzel, R. *Behavior modification in the natural environment.* New York: Academic Press, 1969.

Todd, F. T. Coverant control of self-evaluative responses in the treatment of depression. A new use for an old principle. *Behavior Therapy,* 1972, *3,* 91-94.

Tolman, E. C. Cognitive maps in rats and men. *Psychological Review,* 1948, *55,* 189-208.

Tooley, F. J., & Pratt, S. An experimental procedure for the extinction of smoking behavior. *Psychological Record,* 1967, *17,* 209-218.

Turkewitz, H., O'Leary, S. G., & Ironsmith, G. Generalization and maintenance of appropriate behavior through self-control. *Journal of Consulting and Clinical Psychology,* 1973, *43,* 577-583.

Van Riper, C. *Speech correction: Principles and methods* (5th ed.). Englewood Cliffs, NJ: Prentice-Hall, 1972.

Wallace, J., & Pear, J. J. Self-control techniques of famous novelists. *Journal of Applied Behavior Analysis,* 1977, *10,* 515-525.

Watson, D. L., & Tharp, R. G. *Self-directed behavior: Self-modification for personal adjustment.* Belmont, CA: Brooks-Cole, 1972.

Wolpe, J. The systematic desensitization treatment of neuroses. *Journal of Nervous and Mental Disease,* 1961, *132,* 189-203.

Wolpe, J. *The practice of behavior therapy.* New York: Pergamon, 1973.

Wolpe, J. *Theme and variations: A behavior therapy casebook.* New York: Pergamon, 1976.

Workman, E. A., Helton, G. B., & Watson, P. J. Self-monitoring effects in a four-year-old child: An ecological behavior analysis. *Journal of School Psychology,* 1982, *20,* 57-64.

Yates, A. J. *Theory and practice in behavior therapy.* New York: Wiley and Sons, 1975.

INDEX

A
Accuracy-38
Adkins, J. L.-118, 122
Aggressive behavior-92, 98, 99
Alberto, P. A.-18-19, 130
Alden, L.-108
Antecedents-17, 27-29, 81-83, 131-132, 134-135, 140-142
Anton, J. L.-108
Anxiety-108
Assessment-7
Assignment completion-74
Atkinson, B.-53

B
Baer, D.-90
Ballard, K. D.-7, 81-83
Bailey, J.-7
Barkley, R. A.-71-72
Barrios, B.-108
Baseline data-7, 14
Bates, D. F.-12
Bates, S.-12
Beck, A. T.-108
Behavior
  analysis-8
  antecedents of-14, 17, 27-29, 81-83,131-132, 134-135, 140-142
  consequences of-13, 17, 24-27, 130-132, 134, 139
  contracting-132, 139
  counting devices-33-36
  covert-105
  disordered-59
  maintenance of-15
  modeling of-14
  generalization of-14-15, 109
  reactivity of-7, 22-23, 45, 70, 97, 106, 107
  recording of-7, 14, 17-19, 20, 22, 33-36, 38, 45-46, 49, 61, 70-73, 85, 94-95,110-111, 119, 120, 129, 138 (see also self-recording, self-evaluation, self-observation)
Behavior analysis-8
Behavioral programming-6
Behavior disordered-59
Behaviors
  aggressive-92, 93-99
  covert-105
  depression-108
  disruptive-91-92
  fear (phobias)-93, 108
  fighting-100, 101
  handwriting-79-81
  mathematics-75-76, 84-86
  personal-105
  phonics-74-75
  reading-86-89
  self-help-122-125
  showering-122-123
  study-77-78
  talking-out-97
  tantrum-93
  teacher-pleasing-133
  unassertive-128
  vocational-118-122
  writing-81-84
Bennett, A.-84
Bernstein, D. A.-101-102
Biglan, A.-108
Boag, P. G.-53
Borkovec, T. D.-101-102

Bornstein, P. H.-7, 28
Brigham, T.-7
Broden, M.-72-73, 97
Bucher, B.-84-85

C
Cartwright, C. A.-18
Cartwright, G. P.-18
Casey, B.-35
Chilcutt, J.-53
Ciminero, A. R.-34, 35, 107
Cognitive behavior modifiers-106, 133
Communication disorders-57
Congressional Record-61
Consequences-13, 17, 24-27, 130-132, 134, 139
Contingency-14, 87-88
Contingency contracting-132, 139
Contracting-132, 139
Cooper, J. O.-79-81
Copeland, A. P.-71-72
Counting devices-33-36
Covert behaviors-105
Creedon, C. F.-87-88
Csapo, M.-7
Cue-14
 audio-71-72
 for praise-118, 120

D
Data
 collection of-45-46
 definition of-14
Davis, J. K.-7
Daya, J.-108
Depression-108
Dickerson, E. A.-87-88
Disruptive behavior-91-92
Dolnick, M.-93, 98
Drabman, R. S.-110-111

E
Eaton, M. D.-80
Emotional instability-92-97
Emotionally disturbed-59
Environmental programming-6
Evaluative overlays-79-81
Event recording-20, 129, 138
Experimental design-129
Extinction-14

F
Fears-93, 108
Fighting-100-101
Frequency-38
Fremouw, W. J.-108
Friedling, C.-88-89
Friedman, L.-108

G
Generalization-14-15, 109
Gifted and talented-61
Glynn, E. L.-7, 81-83
Goldfried, M. R.-108
Goldiamond, I.-83
Goodman, J.-28, 135
Graphing-40-41, 45, 142-144
Graubard, P. S.-133
Grossman, H. J.-53

H
Hall, R. V.-72-73, 97
Handwriting-79-81
Hannum, J. W.-35
Hansen, C. L.-80
Hearing-impaired-57
Hefferman, T.-77-78
Helton, G. B.-70
Helwig, J. J.-79-81
Hemingway, E.-44, 83, 84
Hering, J.-80
Heward, W. L.-54, 135
Hollon, S.-108
Homme, L.-107
Horner, R. H.-7
Hubbard, D. R.-35
Hugo, V.-84
Hundert, J.-84-85

I
Individualized education plans (IEPs)-52
Ironsmith, G.-93-94, 109
Intensity-38
Interval recording-119
Interval time sampling-20

J
Jackson, H. J.-53
Jacobson, E.-99
Jaynes, J.-134
Johnson, W. B.-107
Jones, J. C.-79-81

Index

K
Kanfer, F. H.-12
Kanter, N. J.-108
Karoly, P.-12
Kauffman, J.-9
Kazdin, A. E.-7, 83
Kovacs. M.-108
Krakochwill, T. R.-9-74
Kunzelman, H. D.-36

L
Latency-38
Layman, R. D.-107
Learning disabled-55-56
Lepper, M. R.-71
Lewinsohn, P. M.-108
Lipinski, D. P.-35, 107
Lobitz, W. C.-105
Lopiccolo, J.-105
Lovitt, T.-80
Lowe, J. E.-105

M
Madsen, C. H.-105
Mahoney, M. J.-6, 35, 36, 107
Maintenance-15
Marchetti, A.-118-122
Marshall, A. E.-135
Mathematics-75-76, 84-86
Matson, J. L.-118, 122
Mayer, G. R.-38, 130
McLaughlin, T. F.-60
McMullen, S.-105
Meichenbaum, D. H.-28, 106, 107, 133, 135
Mentally retarded 53-55
Mikulas, W. L.-105
Miller, M. B.-133
Millham, J.-53
Mitts, B.-72-73, 97
Modeling-14

N
Nathan, M.-53
Negative practice-113
Nelson, R. O.-35, 107
Norman, J. E.-79-81

O
O'Brien, F.-35
O'Leary, S. G.-7, 88-89

Operational definition-17-19, 129, 136-137
Orlansky, M. D.-53

P
Patterson, C. J.-71
Peacock, R.-107
Pear, J. J.-83-84
Peer reinforcement-133
Permanent product recording-19-20
Personal behaviors-105
Phobias-93
Phonics-74-75
Physically disabled-58
Piersall, W. C.-9, 74
P. L.-94-142-55
Polsgrove, L.-60
Powell, J.-35
Pratt, S.-107
Punisher, W. C.-9, 74

Q
Quevillon, R. P.-7, 28

R
Radical behaviorist-106, 133
Rand, D. C.-8
Reactivity-7, 22-23, 45, 70, 97, 106, 107
Reading-74-75, 86-89
Recording mechanisms-33-36
Recording techniques-138
Reinforcer-13-14, 25, 99, 133, 139
Reisman, J. M.-35
Relaxation training-93
Relaxation technique-101-102
Reliability-22, 49, 61, 110-111
  incentives for-85-94-95, 120
Response cost-139
Richards, C. S.-77-78
Richard, H. C.-107
Robin, A.-93-98, 103
Role playing-93-99
Roll, D.-35
Rosen, R. C.-105
Rosenbaum, M. S.-110-111
Rosenberg, H.-133
Rubin, H.-35
Ruppel, G.-86-87
Rush, A. J.-108

S
Safran, J.-108

Sagotsky, G.-71
Schneider, M.-93-98
Schulmann, J. L.-35
Self-evaluation-21, 94-95, 113, 124, 129, 138
Self-help skills-122-125
Self-instruction-27-29, 88-89, 107-108, 135
Self-observation-6, 13
Self-rating-94-95, 97
Self-recording-6-13
Self-reinforcement-134
Setting-14
Seymour, F. W.-7, 117, 118
Shee, S. M.-7
Sheehan, D. J.-35
Showering skills-122-123
Shigetomi, C.-108
Sivage, C.-71-72
Skinner, B. F.-83, 106, 133, 134
Solomon, R. W.-133
Stability of baseline data-40-41
Stimulus change-14
Stimulus control-135, 140-142
Stokes, T. F.-7
Stokes, T. F.-90, 117, 118
Study skills-77-78
Sulzer-Azaroff, B.-38, 130
Swanson, L.-7
Systematic desensitization-93, 101, 108

T
Talkington, J.-108
Talk-outs-97
Target behavior-13, 31-33
Task-analysis-54, 122-123
Task-related behaviors-69-74
Teacher pleasing behaviors-133
Temper tantrums-93
Test anxiety-108
Tharp, R.-7, 47, 108
Therapy-7-8
Thomas, J. D.-7

Thoreson, C. E.-6, 35, 36, 107
Time sampling-20, 70-73, 129, 138
Todd, F. T.-107
Tolman, E. C.-107
Tooley, F. J.-107
Topography-38-39
Trap, J.-79-81
Trollope, A.-84
Troutman, A.-130
Troutman, P. A.-18-19
Turkewitz, H.-93, 94, 109
Turtle technique-93, 99

U
Ullman, L. P.-105
Unassertive behavior-108

V
Van Riper, C.-57
Visual response system-135
Visually impaired-56
Vocational skills-118-122

W
Wahler, R. G.-133
Wallace, J.-83-84
Wardrobe maintenance-123
Watson, D. L.-47, 70, 108
Weideman, R.-108
Wetzel, R.-7
Wolpe, J.-93, 100, 108
Workman, E. A.-70, 71
Written expression-81-84

Y
Yates, A. J.-100, 108

Z
Zeiss, A. M.-108
Zitter, R. E.-108